# HENRY FORD
# "IGNORANT IDEALIST"

Kennikat Press
**National University Publications**
Series in American Studies

# HENRY FORD
## *"Ignorant Idealist"*

### DAVID E. NYE

National University Publications
KENNIKAT PRESS // 1979
Port Washington, N.Y. // London

Manufactured in the United States of America

Published by
**Kennikat Press Corp.**
Port Washington, N. Y. / London

**Library of Congress Cataloging in Publication Data**

Nye, David E     1946–
    Henry Ford, ignorant idealist.

    (National university publications: American
studies series)
    Bibliography: p.
    Includes index.
    1. Ford, Henry, 1863–1947. I. Title.
TL140.F6N93     ~~629.2'092'4~~ [B]        79-464
ISBN 0-8046-9242-4

# CONTENTS

PREFACE      vii

INTRODUCTION      3

**PART ONE: THE WORLD'S VIEW OF HENRY FORD**

1. AN IGNORANT IDEALIST      9
2. COME AND LEAD US OUT      22
3. BREAD AND BULLETS      40

**PART TWO: HENRY FORD'S VIEW OF THE WORLD**

4. I BELONG WITH THE BUDDHIST CROWD      59
5. TO STOP WAR BY DESTROYING COWS      70
6. BY INSTINCT AN ENGINEER      93
7. THE WATCH'S MAINSPRING      106

**PART THREE: PRESERVING NATURE'S ORDER**

8. THE MACHINE IS THE NEW MESSIAH      125

NOTES      132

BIBLIOGRAPHIC ESSAY      139

INDEX      144

# ACKNOWLEDGMENTS

The following read the manuscript and offered helpful advice: Henry Edmunds, Director, Ford Archives; Professors William Hagen, David Stineback, Douglas Lewis, Mary Turpie, Edward Griffin, David Noble, and especially my thesis advisor, Mulford Sibley. I am also indebted to the following libraries and archives: The Wilson Library, University of Minnesota; Detroit Public Library; Archives of Labor History and Urban Affairs, Wayne State University; The Union College Schaffer Library; The National Archives; and especially the Ford Archives in Greenfield Village, whose David Crippen and Winthrop Sears provided invaluable assistance. Special thanks also to Fran and Peggy Shor of Wayne State University, who made my second visit to Detroit more pleasant, my friends in Minnesota who endured this project, and Marjorie Windstone, my typist, who relieved me of the manuscript at the last.

Finally, I thank my grandmother, Margaret L. Drumheller, who supported my research at its inception, and Union College, whose Humanities Development Fund grant allowed me to complete the project.

# PREFACE

Perhaps there is no better introduction to Henry Ford than the city of Dearborn, where he grew up and later built the Rouge Plant, the world's largest industrial unit. For a moment as I drove into Dearborn, I sped along a nearly deserted freeway at dusk, crossing open fields. I passed the looming Willow Run Plant, where Ford had built bombers during the Second World War, and suddenly emerged on one of the four-lane shopping strips that extend for miles outside every American city. Lined with motels, drive-in banks, garages, fast-food restaurants, supermarkets, and other monuments to mass production, this world was shaped and organized to the demands of the automobile.

Ford's favorite author, Ralph Waldo Emerson, once declared that "An institution is the lengthened shadow of one man," concluding that "all history resolves itself very easily into the biography of a few stout and earnest persons." In a sense the world of the freeway is Henry Ford's shadow. The highways where men assemble their desires in chains of services are an immense assembly line, where men move themselves along the line.

One fact was clear: Ford was far more than a symbolic figure. He had acted upon the world as had few others in history. His determination to produce an inexpensive car for the millions was a fundamental innovation, along with the assembly line, which seemed so simple in retrospect that, like the wheel, it appeared inevitable. Yet some societies never used the wheel, and in the twentieth century other great nations have emerged without relying so heavily upon the automobile, and not merely because they were less wealthy, but because they espoused different values. Despite Ford's undeniable world influence, especially in Russia, it seems likely that future societies will not organize so completely around the automobile, especially in light of the developing ecological crisis and fuel shortage. Yet even before that crisis, which the automobile hastened, the highly industrialized European cities were of quite a different character than American metropolises, which had little affinity with the Latin words which once linked cities with the citizen, the urbane, and civility.

For, to return to Dearborn, its organization of life reduces the landscape to a two-dimensional scheme, and while driving, Americans can no more converse than they can walk to work, smelling the morning air. All necessities are separated by automotive distances. In my own case, I slept twenty-five freeway minutes from Greenfield Village, where I did my research. I ate two miles from my motel and had my muffler repaired at a gas station near the motel, but across the six-lane freeway. After leaving the car, I had to dodge through the heavy traffic to the neutral zone of the median strip, where I waited amid the rumbling of trucks and the rush of cars until somewhere a distant traffic light created a ripple of silence, and I crossed the warm pavement, trotting into the motel driveway. Later, trucks would disturb my sleep. Appropriately, it would have been impossible to do research at the Ford Archives without owning an automobile. (Inappropriately, I drove a ten-year-old Chevrolet.)

As I sat in a fast-food restaurant at twilight, exhausted from my long drive, eating food identical to dinners being served from Texas to Anchorage, I knew that my life, American life, was somehow wrapped up with that of Henry Ford. And yet, what do we know of him? In previous months I had learned to my surprise that the man who said history was bunk also read Emerson, Tolstoy, and Carlyle, enjoyed close friendships with John Burroughs and Thomas Edison, coauthored five books, and possessed a personal library of over two thousand volumes. While not an intellectual in the conventional sense, Ford was hardly just another engineer who had invented a useful gadget. He speculated and acted in the realms of politics, economics, religion, and of course, business. Even more surprising, his ideas were more systematic than his critics or even his friends had guessed.

In Dearborn I would try to locate the center of that system, which appeared to be but a collection of anachronisms from the nineteenth century. Yet one had only to glimpse the incongruous juxtaposition of Greenfield Village with the nearby Rouge River Plant to know that however outdated Ford's ideas appeared, they expressed themselves in more than antiquarian pursuits. But where was the source of that gigantic force? That was a mystery, and like all great mysteries had defenses, one of which was the innocuous-looking collection of buildings Ford had gathered to form Greenfield Village. But the greatest defense of all was the overwhelming presence of multifaceted power in the sprawling freeway systems and their conveyor-belts of automobiles passing the automated banks and stores, in the organization of every facility for mass production, and in the rows of duplicate houses that stretched through the suburban night.

The environment which had spread from Ford's factories across America was like a seal which could never be broken, and it seemed that the nature of this power might be sought only at its origin. Elsewhere the power Ford had unleashed was everywhere too naked and overwhelming to be grasped. Rather, one acceded to it everywhere, whether in rush-hour traffic or a suburban home. Only in the replica of Independence Hall and that supermarket of history Ford had preserved in Greenfield Village could one suddenly apprehend something of the forces everywhere at work. Here he had assembled the past he found significant, the homes he knew, and the life he revered. Here lay that part of him which had done more than create automobiles.

# HENRY FORD
# "IGNORANT IDEALIST"

# ABOUT THE AUTHOR

David E. Nye is Director of American Studies at Union College in Schenectady, New York. He has been a Fulbright Professor in Spain, and is the author of various articles in scholarly journals.

# INTRODUCTION

Henry Ford was one of the most popular Americans in our history. In what sense was he representative? And of what? To an extent he was an ideal type made flesh, embodying the creed of self-reliance, the frontier myth, and the Alger story. However, I have chosen not to define him as an ideal type. Previous scholars working in the symbol-myth tradition of American Studies have tended toward defining a symbol as "an image which embodies an idea."[1] But this straightforward functionalism does not recognize the ambiguous quality of symbols. In Greek *symbolon* is formed from words meaning "thrown" and "together" and means "a sign or token." A symbol is thus a token which puts together a number of elements and contains them. Rather than representing a single idea, a symbol is a kind of cultural shorthand, compressing ideas, values, and expectations into a convenient, abbreviated form. In this view a symbol is prone to instability and ambiguity, and a symbolic figure necessarily is one whose meanings prove to be flexible and protean.

An analysis of Henry Ford's public life reveals such a symbolic figure, one who lived a series of mythic lives. The public continually recast his meaning, selecting and shifting the elements of his life. The Ford of the 1930's bore but passing resemblance to the figure of the 1920's, for example, although they necessarily were composed of similar elements. Ford existed as a screen, receiving psychological projections from society. Rather than embodying an idea, he existed for the public as a malleable

bundle of contradictions ambiguous enough to admit of many interpretations according to the needs of the moment.

To determine Ford's public images I have examined polls, newspapers, magazines, popular biographies, and other materials such as
cartoons, songs, and the ubiquitous Ford jokes. I have relied particularly on popular magazines, in line with Theodore P. Green's argument
in *America's Heroes* that magazines were national forums whose success depended upon their ability to satisfy a general audience: "More
far-ranging and reflective than the newspaper, more immediately
responsive to change than the school book, more continuous than the
best-selling book, the general magazine offers . . . one of the more
promising indexes to change in national values." The magazine articles concerning Ford over a thirty-five year period provided a context
for other materials which reflected his various public images.

The structure of Ford's images records a growing awareness of the
conflict between the nineteenth-century vision of America as an
Edenic democracy and the twentieth-century realities of industrialization and urbanization. The single most important function of these
images, however, was to reassure Americans that industrialism was in
fundamental harmony with their vision of a developing pastoral
utopia.

That earlier vision had been articulated through the symbol of
Andrew Jackson. In his seminal study, John William Ward concluded
that "To describe the early nineteenth century as the age of Jackson
misstates the matter. The age was not his. He was the age's."[2] But,
one might object, Jackson was a consummate politician; he cultivated
the myth which grew up around him and usually acted in accordance
with it. A comparison with Ford is instructive. Ford became not one,
but several symbols, over time. Furthermore, as a private citizen, he
had less need of public approbation than the politicians who have often
been studied as symbolic figures, and many of his actions, such as the
abortive Peace Ship expedition or his anti-Semitic attacks, were not
calculated to harmonize with a public image. Like his belief in reincarnation, they expressed a personal vision, but one which the public chose
repeatedly to ignore.

Because of this discrepancy between the public and private Ford, one
may dismiss the argument that his image was based merely on a response
to his actions, especially since Ford made considerable efforts to make
his views known. A stimulus-response model is too simple to explain

why the public chose to distort the events of his career or simply ignored some of his public statements and instead constructed other
images. I have not argued, however, that Ford was an archetype of the
collective unconscious or an externalization of subconscious needs.
Such arguments are based on an early anthropology and have been
challenged. However useful Sigmund Freud and Carl Jung may be in
individual analysis, they both presuppose a teleology that implicitly
denigrates archaic society. The works of Mircea Eliade and Claude
Levi-Strauss force modern man to recognize the sophistication of the
so-called "primitive," making him a contemporary rather than an antecedent.[3] They also make evolutionary theories of consciousness suspect. We are linked to archaic societies not by psychic evolution but
by similarities of structure and psychological need, and with these
linkages in mind I have approached Henry Ford's position in American
culture. Although influenced by Levi-Strauss and Eliade, however, I
am neither's disciple, and wish to stress that they have been influences
only. I have not adopted either's methods or terminology wholesale.

To complement the study of the structure of Ford's images I also
examine the structure of his world view. Previous commentators have
argued that Ford's was an eccentric and whimsical nature, which made
him unpredictable, especially outside his business. However, an underlying system in his thinking emerges once freed from the misconcep-
tions of his contemporaries. By regarding Ford's actions as expressions
of religious ideas, such apparently unrelated subjects as dietary theory
and the assembly line merge in a larger design articulating his belief
in reincarnation. I have resisted the temptation to explain this organizing principle as part of an Oedipus complex. How this might have
been done will be obvious in the text, but such reductionism would
efface the importance of Ford's conscious thoughts and actions. It
would also suggest that reincarnation was implausible and illegitimate,
and while I do not accept the theory, it would be far too ethnocentric
to dismiss it as delusion or fixation.

By analyzing the structure of both Ford's public images and his
private world view something of the essential character of culture
emerges. Social reality is not a something lurking behind public symbols
and private views. It is not an "actual" disconnected from the perceptions of human beings. Rather, the coalescence of the public and the
private, the corporate and the individual, creates a society's tensions
and meanings. The categories of public thought and Ford's world view,

while different, reflected the difficulties which confronted twentieth-century American culture. They exhibit parallel structures; each tried to synthesize nineteenth-century agrarian individualism with the emerging industrialism, envisioning a world in danger, but one which might be salvaged. Their common utopian impulse ultimately justifies the view that symbols and myths shape historical events far beyond demands of material circumstances, that men and women act not only from pettiness and self-interest, but also out of a vision of change, however misguided their dreams.

# PART 1

# THE WORLD'S VIEW OF HENRY FORD

*"A great man is a new statue in every attitude and action."*

Marked by Henry Ford in Emerson's "Art"

*"To be great is to misunderstood."*

Emerson, "Self Reliance"

*CHAPTER ONE*

# AN IGNORANT IDEALIST

In the first half of the twentieth century, Henry Ford was America's greatest hero. A farmer's son, he had become an inventor, and without special privileges or inherited wealth created a billion-dollar industry which also contributed to the national welfare. No wonder he was more widely publicized than any other private citizen. Only presidents were assured of more headlines. For a generation Ford's factory was besieged as though it were the industrial White House by reporters on permanent assignments. Around the globe in New Zealand schoolboys thought him one of the three greatest men in the world. Model T's carried his fame to China. Ford was a hero to Germans and Russians, and his factories were established on every inhabited continent. He made half the world's automobiles.

If Ford loomed large in the world's imagination, he became the dominant American of his times. His actions were all of epic proportions, as he tamed rivers, constructed fleets of ships, established the first regular airline, built the world's largest industrial plant, and manufactured 15,000,000 Model T's. Yet despite these accomplishments he seemed as full of strange quirks and idiosyncracies as a Michigan farmer. A self-educated man, he opposed jazz, smoking, drinking, and city ways. His life seemed to incorporate the national experience—from the frontier, where his father had settled, to the new industrial nation that he helped to build in the twentieth century.

Because Ford's life seemed to recapitulate the national experience, because he was the immigrant's son become industrial titan, he proved uniquely suited to act as a symbolic figure. He lived as a symbol in the social contexts of war, boom, and depression, illustrating rapid changes in American life. He was not the symbol of an unchanging order, yet he incorporated the values of the past.

Throughout the nineteenth century, Americans prized self-help and maintained that character alone determined success. They lionized a Franklin and extolled the virtues of a Lincoln because each apparently founded his success upon superlative character rather than special privilege, training, or luck. By 1830 Americans had yoked this emphasis on character with a belief in the beneficent power of nature to inspire and nurture genius. This fusion crystallized in the figure of the backwoodsman, found proof in the victory of American militia over trained British troops at New Orleans, and presented Andrew Jackson as an ideal. The triumph of "untutored genius" on the battlefield became a symbolic episode in the formation of the American character and helped spawn a log-cabin tradition which demanded that all great Americans be born (or claim to have been born) in ennobled poverty.

The advent of industrialization, however, forced a change in the typology of American heroes. Increasingly, social mobility was substituted for geographical mobility. The self-made man might begin life on the farm, but rose to success in an urban world. Success manuals stressed that upper-class birth usually impeded advancement, since sturdy character and unswerving purpose were not easily cultivated among the idle rich. Character rather than privilege, hard work rather than brilliance, were the attributes necessary for success. Given these, the American was told, he could not fail to rise.

In actuality, however, there was more poverty than progress and, typically, a modest mobility from the level of unskilled laborer to the semiskilled level, with perhaps an occasional advance to trade. Only a handful of industrialists rose to great wealth, and their methods, if Jay Gould and John D. Rockefeller were any sample, hardly confirmed popular myths. If there were acres of diamonds, they were for the few.[1]

The contrast between ideal and reality emerged at another level when Frederick Jackson Turner formulated his "Frontier Thesis," which noted the passing of the frontier as a category in the 1890 census and asserted that American character had been the unique product of contact between European civilization and the New World. Running through Turner's famous address and through the public discourse of the new century were new questions: How could Americans preserve their character without nature? What would prevent them from sliding into decay and European degeneration in a few generations? The problem had many manifestations, from muckraking articles against slum conditions, the eventual triumph of anti-immigration forces, the National Parks movement, the sudden emergence of a new popular western literature exalting the lost frontier, and an accelerating trend toward suburban living.

But the one logical response was missing. The crisis in American ideology did not lead to attacks upon industrialism for destroying the natural world, vitiating the national character, and modifying beyond recognition the conditions for success. In fact, Americans embraced industrialization and soon would see in Henry Ford a symbolic resolution to the difficulties their ideology imposed.

In the century's first decade Ford was known only to automotive enthusiasts. His was not the first American car; nor was it at first the cheapest or the best. He was simply another of the many tinkerers who found financial backing, and his cars were assembled from parts produced by local machine shops. The horseless carriage itself was a European invention, as the names of its parts indicate. "Automobile," "radiator," and "carburetor," for example, all came from the French. As in Europe, the early enthusiasts were mostly wealthy men willing to spend large sums for machines that might occasionally even work, but which they did not rely upon for transportation.

To the general public cars did not seem terribly important after the initial sensation they created. In fact, 1896 photographs of Detroit street scenes reveal that most people ignored one of the few motor cars in the city, as it wove its way between pedestrians and wagons.[2] Few conceived of the automobile as the center of American industry; few discussed the changes it might bring.

Both this general obliviousness to the importance of the automobile and Ford's position as one of hundreds involved in its initial development precluded early fame. Local newspapers wrote about his car once it was completed, but their coverage was hardly extravagant. Ford was regarded as an ordinary citizen, perhaps a little obsessed with his hobby.

National attention first came in 1902, after Barney Oldfield set a speed record driving Ford's "999," a car built for the race, which beat three others as it sped over the five-mile track in five minutes and twenty-eight seconds, an American record. Oldfield, a former bicycle racer, received nearly as much publicity as Ford, whose fame in this instance was ephemeral. Even after he had become a major industrialist he was generally ignored. Before 1913 he would not even be listed in the *International Who's Who,* although by then he was the world's largest producer of automobiles.

Only in a more indirect way did the race aid Ford's career: by encouraging investors to contribute to the formation of the Ford Motor Company. Previously Ford had unsuccessfully designed a car for the Detroit Automobile Company and had also been retained by a few of the backers of that company once it dissolved. Thus the racing coup was needed before new money could be attracted. In the months after the race, nine stockholders joined with a coal dealer, Alexander Malcomson, and his chief clerk, James Couzens, to back the new venture. Together they invested only $28,000. Stock was distributed both for this cash investment and also in return for machinery and patents. Ford put no money into the venture, but received 255 of the 1,000 shares of stock. Thus initially Ford did not control the company which bore his name.

Generally, automobile stock was not considered a solid investment, but a highly speculative one, even when profitable. This is illustrated by John Gray, the second-largest investor in the Ford Motor Company. After the first three years, in which he had received a 500% return on his investment, Gray wanted to sell his stock. He retained it, however, because "he could not in full honesty recommend to any of his friends that they buy it. He said solemnly: 'This business cannot last.'"[3] Gray's doubts were but a single instance of the common suspicion that automobiles were only a fad and their stocks high risks. The future impact of the car was not generally foreseen, even by those who had profited from its production, and consequently the early automotive inventors were joked about for their impracticality as much as they were respected for mechanical ingenuity.

The inventors themselves were more prescient. In fact, one of the best-known early inventors never constructed a car, but instead organized a monopoly. George Selden, a mechanically minded lawyer, had taken out a comprehensive patent on a motor car in May 1879. Unable to find financial backing, he attempted to control automotive production through his legal skills. The result was the Association of Licensed Automobile Manufacturers (ALAM), which eventually included most of the major companies except Ford's and which forced them to pay a percentage to the patent holders. The ALAM tried to force Ford to join, but he responded with a long legal battle which began in 1903 and lasted until January 1911, at a cost of $500,000 to both sides. But the stakes were even higher—millions would accrue to the victor.

When Ford won, the ALAM disappeared within a year, as the smaller companies who had joined out of fear refused to remain members. This fight against monopoly during the "trust busting" days of Teddy Roosevelt brought Ford some fame. However, it was based upon a complex legal argument over the nature of engines which even the judges found hard to follow.

In contrast, Ford's announcement of the Five Dollar Day in January 1914 directly affected the life of every working American. Ford's announcement that he would pay every one of his workers five dollars a day was a front-page headline in every American city, because he was doubling wages overnight. His workers had not asked that their pay be increased, and he had no shortage of employees, yet Ford voluntarily distributed $10,000,000 of his profits.

Public response was overwhelming. The *New York Times* alone carried over thirty stories dealing with Ford in the next three months, and Ford virtually canceled all advertising during the next five years, as he found his free publicity created demand for more automobiles than he could make. Part of the fascination with the Five Dollar Day stemmed from its apparent impossibility. Many questioned whether the generosity was wise, since other workers might demand similar wages in industries where they could not be paid. The conservative *Wall Street Journal* declared that Henry Ford was a menace who had "in his social endeavors committed economic blunders, if not crimes . . . [which] . . . may return to plague him and the industry he represents, as well as organized society." The inequality that Ford's high wages created might lead to instability. The very plethora which made Ford's high wages possible might underscore the comparative poverty of others.

Half a century of labor unrest was conjured up as reason enough not to suddenly overpay workers. But while the *New York Times* believed that "strikes are likely enough, and conditions of peace cannot be looked for," many other newspapers and the vast majority of the working public were ecstatic. The *New York Globe* lauded the plan and thought it might lead to profit-sharing in other factories. The *New York World* felt Ford had made "a step toward the stewardship of industrial welfare on the part of employers. . . . In effect, the Ford Company has made its workmen stockholders." Similarly, across the nation newspapers heralded a new partnership of capital and labor.[4]

The socialist *New York Daily People* attacked the plan, however, calling it a $10,000,000 dust-raising scheme designed to ruin competitors. Ford's act was compared to Carnegie's earlier manipulation of the price of steel through tariffs, which had enabled him to consolidate his holdings under high tariffs and then drive competitors from the field by lowering the price. Similarly, the paper suspected that later Ford might slash wages and drive competitors to the wall.

Ford was thus attacked by both conservatives and socialists. Neither they nor the general public understood the principles of the assembly line, which made the new high wage possible. Yet perfection of the moving assembly line antedated the new wage policy. In the summer of 1913 average chassis assembly time had been twelve and one-half man-hours. Then operations were meticulously studied, timed, and divided into small work units, and machinery was installed to do much of the heavy labor. Moving belts were installed wherever possible to bring the parts to the worker at the ideal height, and operations were organized in sequence along the belts. Chassis assembly time first was cut in half, and then further reduced to one hour and thirty-three minutes. A procedure which had previously required 750 minutes now took less than 100. Labor costs dropped accordingly, although somewhat offset by investments in new machinery.

The saving, however, was still prodigious and made the new wage possible. But because few understood or even knew about the assembly line, Ford's Five Dollar Day seemed outrageous to some, and to many he naturally appeared sympathetic and intriguing but too much guided by his heart rather than by his head. Only after the shock of the announcement had worn off did the basis of the high wage gradually become comprehensible. The most popular exhibit at the 1915 Panama Pacific Exposition was an operating assembly line, where crowds watched automobiles being created before their eyes. In Detroit, visitors poured through the Highland Park Plant, where the Model T's came off the assembly line in droves. Those who wished detailed information found the techniques explained in *Ford Methods and Ford Shops,* which became a handbook to other industrialists.[5]

Within the business community, the ultimate test of high wages was profits, and the Ford Motor Company passed that test with profits of $30,000,000; $24,000,000; and $60,000,000 from 1914 to 1916. In addition to the time saved on the assembly line, Ford profited from the reduction in labor turnover and the ability of workers to buy Model T's themselves. Many would eventually see this as Ford's greatest contribution: he made the worker into a consumer, sustaining prosperity for capital and labor as a result.

Had Ford done nothing more, his fame would have been secure. The double achievement of the assembly line and the Five Dollar Day, not to mention his popular motor car, made him an American hero. In 1914 he was fifty-one. He had worked hard until his company achieved an incredible success. His original stockholders had received even more on their initial investment than those who had shared in the fabled British East India Company, and Ford, who owned a majority of the stock, was rumored to be one of the wealthiest men in the world. A benevolent man, he combined science and generosity in his production of an inexpensive and reliable car. He was a champion of free enterprise who had risen from humble origins. What more perfect ingredients for an American hero?

But before the unsettling announcement of the Five Dollar Day could be vindicated and before the elements of Ford's image could coalesce, World War I began, temporarily dividing the public until entry into the war silenced political dissent. Ford's own reactions to the war mirrored changes in the public mood. While the nation espoused neutrality, Ford launched a crusade for peace which confused admirers, vindicated critics, and aroused more laughter than anything else. Upset with the carnage of the war, in 1915 Ford declared to a young reporter, "I hate war, because war is murder, desolation, and destruction, causeless, unjustifiable, cruel and heartless to those of the human race who do not want it, the countless millions, the workers. I hate it none the less for its waste, its uselessness, and the barriers it raises against progress."[6] His words appeared in most of the national papers, and while such sentiments were extreme, they did reflect America's initial unwillingness to take sides and a national sense of the insanity of war.

However, sympathy for the Allies grew almost daily through 1915. By December when Ford announced that he would try to stop the war through personal mediation, by sailing a "Peace Ship" to Europe, the press refused to take the plan seriously and ridiculed him in humorous stories and cartoons. They jeered at his boast that he would "get the boys out of the trenches by Christmas." He was called "The Jason of the Peace Argonauts," "a wise maniac," and "quixotic." The expedition itself was dubbed "Ford's Folly," "a wild goose chase," "the peace joy ride," "more innocents abroad," and a "jitney peace excursion." As in the issue of the Five Dollar Day, moreover, Ford was seldom attacked for his motives. The *Boston Transcript* declared, the plan "does his heart and soul more credit than it does his head. . . ." The expedition was "a beautiful piece of idealism," but the paper advised Ford to send his money to the wounded.[7]

While Ford's expedition failed, it did add another facet to his character and allowed Americans of many regions and political persuasions to identify with some aspect of his character. William Jennings Bryan, leader of the Populist movement, was also against the war, and Ford met him briefly in New York shortly before embarking. Already because of his rural origins, his promise to produce a farm tractor, and of course his Model T, Ford had emerged as a folk hero.[8] His Flivver made transportation easy and assumed such farm chores as sawing wood, hauling produce, and pumping water. Conversion kits were even available to adapt the car to plow fields. To the rural American, Ford signified progress, success, and self-reliance, and because of his pacifism and antipathy to bankers, he seemed an unreconstructed Populist.

To others Ford appeared a Wilsonian liberal, however, including the president himself. Ford's unexpected primary victories in Nebraska, Michigan, and Missouri led Wilson to ask Ford to run for the Senate seat from Michigan in 1918, and Ford agreed. But he refused to make campaign appearances and lost to Truman Newberry in a close race. Just as Wilson had won reelection on the slogan "He kept us out of war" and then entered the fray, by 1918 Ford, who once had sworn to burn his factory to the ground rather than let it be used for arms production, offered to mass produce a thousand submarines a day and made the extravagant promise that he would not keep a penny of war profits.

Both Ford and Wilson mirrored the changing national mood. Ford reflected a growing tendency to identify business interests with the national welfare. As America entered the war a new industrial hero appeared in the national magazines. The progressive emphasis on individualism, the attempt to separate private and public interests, and the muckraking attitude toward business were all submerged in wartime cooperation and a frenzied patriotism. The new industrial heroes were efficient managers who emphasized cooperation and attended to detail.[9] Ford epitomized these tendencies with his rationalized production system, the principle of the assembly line, and the Five Dollar Day—which together assured national prosperity and wartime efficiency.

Ford's appeal lay in an amalgam of managerial expertise, humble origins, and an idiosyncratic individualism which did not interfere with wartime collectivism. The Peace Ship confirmed his eccentricity, but his good intentions were clear. In crisis he responded to the nation's need, and if the rashness of his actions undercut the apparent infallibility of his earlier industrial success, Ford became more human to other Americans, although still he seemed a bit of a mystery. His character was clarified, however, by a bizarre trial.

In 1916 the *Chicago Tribune,* suspicious of Ford's patriotism, accused him of being an anarchist. Ford responded with a $1,000,000 libel suit which, due to an error of his lawyers, focused on the entire content of the *Tribune*'s editorial rather than on the single word "anarchist." That word alone had proven grounds for libel in the past, and had the Ford attorneys been content with it, the case might have been won easily, especially with the "Red Scare" fresh in the public mind when the trial began in May 1919 at Mt. Clements, Michigan.

However, the *Tribune* had also called Ford ignorant, and it quickly became apparent that its lawyers would try to prove it by putting Ford on the witness stand. A courthouse packed with reporters made Ford's blunders famous for years, confirming suspicions that he was a typical rural American. He was unable to define "commenced," "chile con carne," or "ballyhoo." He asserted that the date of the American Revolution was 1812, and when asked to identify Benedict Arnold, replied, "He is a writer, I guess."

Gleefully, many pounced on such testimony. The *Nation* concluded:

The mystery is finally dispelled. Henry Ford is a Yankee mechanic pure and simple, quite uneducated, with a mind unable to "bite" into any proposition outside of his automobile and tractor business, but with naturally good instincts and some sagacity. Enter any one of the great factories that line the railroad between New York and Boston and you will find a dozen foremen just like Henry Ford, save that Fortune has poured no unending golden stream into their laps. Many of them are better educated; many of them have far more sagacity.

From the *Nation*'s elitist perspective Ford was merely a common man whose success could be attributed to luck. But a middle-brow magazine such as the *Literary Digest* defended Ford with precisely the same tools that the *Nation* used to reduce him in stature. The *Digest* defended his ignorance, contending that "the grilling of Henry Ford" revealed only that he forgot the inessential information which all schoolboys forget. He was a typical American, whose hard work and attention to a single task had made him successful. In other words, Ford's life fit the description of the nineteenth-century success manual, which stressed character and diligence rather than genius or special privilege. The *Digest* also praised Ford for his idealism, and even the *Nation* admitted that "he injured nobody and drove nobody out of business."

But Ford did not need other defenders. He had protected himself under cross-examination well enough on occasion. When asked, "What was the United States originally?" Ford had slowly replied, "Land, I guess." At another point, when baffled by some obscurity, he had snapped, "I could find a man in five minutes who could tell me all about it." Usually, however, Ford remained calm, and often seemed bored by the proceedings, looking out the courtroom windows or whittling on the sole of his shoe with a pocket knife, until he finally called himself "an ignorant idealist." Naturally the defense seized upon this admission as a substantiation of the *Tribune*'s "libel."

The phrase "ignorant idealist" was also picked up by the popular press, and Arthur Brisbane's syndicated column in the Hearst newspapers suggested that Ford's confession of ignorance was the mark of real wisdom. More ignorance of the same kind was what America needed. Brisbane called upon his readers to write Ford.

If busy with your crops, cut this out and mail it with your name signed: "Dear Ford: I am glad to have you for a fellow citizen and I wish we had more of your brand of anarchism, if that is what it is. Yours truly: Sign here_____."

*Chicago Herald,* July 16, 1919

As Wik reports, "thousands responded by clipping out the editorial and attaching it to their letters" in a dramatic illustration of Ford's popular appeal. Brisbane's column and its response demonstrate that Ford's libel suit had been transformed into a vindication of the common man.[10]

When the trial ended—Ford won and received six cents in damages— he was an enigma no longer. Americans thought he had been unveiled, and they debated over what they saw. To most he signified themselves writ large, a man of the people who had risen to great wealth through hard work. Nor had he forgotten his origins. He was building tractors and cars for the average citizen, lowering their prices yearly, and paying his workers higher wages. If he lacked formal education, so much the better. He seemed simple and straightforward in a world grown increasingly complex. His car could be fixed by anyone and didn't require expensive expert help. He was a second-generation immigrant, son of the soil, hard-working, white, Christian, idealistic, well-meaning.

To the educated minority, Ford was all of these things, but less. He was ignorant, changeable, precipitous in action, and sometimes relied too much on his heart rather than his head. Although his Five Dollar Day had proven itself, the announcement had been inflammatory and should have been privately prepared for. Although the Peace Ship had done no harm, it was still a quixotic expedition at best, which might have had grave consequences.

But beyond these evaluations, Ford had a rustic charm all his own. Americans affectionately joked about him and the Model T, to the point where a whole literature of Ford jokebooks emerged[11] and vaudeville comedians made Tin Lizzie humor a part of their repertoire. Analysis of these jokes reveals how the car's image reenforced the image of its inventor. Many played upon the Model T's plainness, commonness, or supposed inferiority in the eyes of the owners of more luxurious cars. Such humor obviously reenforced the idea that Ford was a representative common man. The archetypal joke of this type is surely that which told of Henry Ford being offered $1.50 for repairing a car stalled along a country road. When Ford declined the money saying he had plenty, the owner called him a liar, "Because if you had plenty of money you'd take some of it and buy yourself an 'automobile' instead of the Ford you're driving."

Other Ford jokes celebrated the car's dependability. A Model T assembled without an engine ran for a month—on its reputation. Cadillac owners carried Lizzies in their tool boxes to pull them out of ditches. The jokes which exaggerated the car's diminutiveness formed a whole class by themselves. They might be delivered by postmen, found in garbage cans, carried in a vest pocket, or painted yellow and sold in bunches at the corner grocery. Such jokes minimized the machine's impact. While in fact the automobile was transforming the face of America, Ford jokes made the car a companion, a rather cantankerous but ladylike bundle of tin which might be fixed with bailing wire.

No other industrialist made a product that aroused similar affection or touched Americans so obviously or directly, and neither Carnegie nor Rockefeller had Ford's appeal. Between 1914 and 1920 Ford received five times more publicity in print than Charlie Chaplin or Mary Pickford, and only Wilson, Bryan, Hughes, and Teddy Roosevelt had more.[12] Ford alone had a distinct class of jokes reserved for him, and if there were some way to measure his impact beyond the printed word, he might surpass all others.

Ford's folksy and approachable image was further enhanced by the wide publicity which accompanied his yearly vacations. In 1915 he had motored through California with Edison, visiting Luther Burbank. From this beginning grew a tradition of yearly vacations with John Burroughs, the naturalist, and Harvey Firestone. All four spent ten days in the Smokies in 1918 and in the Adirondacks the next year. Many newspapers followed the trips, emphasizing their simplicity and camaraderie. A modern historian summarized these reports.

Here were he-men roughing it amid the wilds of nature. Candid camera shots revealed such exciting events as Edison sleeping under a tree, or the elderly John Burroughs beating Ford in a tree chopping contest. Rumors had Ford taking dips in a creek stark naked, and that Burroughs added to scientific knowledge by demonstrating that a skunk could be carried by his tail without dangerous repercussions.

Through such accounts Ford became wrapped in a glow of simplicity and even boyishness. Footracing, berry-picking, roughing it far off the beaten track, Ford harkened back to the nineteenth century, Huck Finn, and the by-gone era of wilderness. His image contrasted sharply with the strikes, Palmer raids, bootlegging, and crime of the postwar years. In an age when Harding was elected on the slogan "Back to Normalcy" Ford's jaunt back to nature was appealing. It suggested that great Americans were like the men in the street. Harding was a composite Lion-Oddfellow-Booster, a comfortable and familiar figure, while Ford appeared to be a likeable farm boy who had made good. As if to cement this identity with the common man, in 1921 Harding joined the Ford camping party, in what one magazine billed as "Four Big Men Become Boys Again."[13]

So Ford became more comprehensible to the average American as he appeared to be more like him. If he had been reduced to the level of a hard-working mechanic, then all Americans who worked as hard might hope for similar luck. If he was no genius, then all might identify with his achievement and feel it their own. If his industry had not corrupted him, it would not corrupt the nation.

# CHAPTER TWO

# COME AND LEAD US OUT

Traditional interpretations of the 1920's such as *Only Yesterday* reflect a belief that the reform impulses which dominated American politics at the turn of the century died in the Great War. More recent interpreters have called the 1920's a "seedtime for reform" and its generation "nervous," noting that the period was a time of uneasiness as much as it was the "era of wonderful nonsense."[1] Yet while there was a reform impulse alive in these years, it did not capture center stage in American life. The laissez-faire ideal and individualism enjoyed a revival under Presidents Harding, Coolidge, and Hoover, who assumed that what was good for business was good for the culture. This belief was not merely the crass commercialism it appeared to be to the critics who compiled *Civilization in the United States,* an indictment of American life as a fruitless materialism. Most Americans believed a spiritual regeneration could be achieved through commerce. Although a writer like Fitzgerald sensed the moral bankruptcy of that vision, although a Hemingway recognized the impotence of money, most of their contemporaries did not.[2]

At the moment of victory in 1918, a religious millennium briefly seemed possible. As Robert Handy found, *A Christian America* and a regeneration of civilization became the focus of crusading churchmen as they emerged from the war. But what started as a massive Interchurch World Movement failed. Simultaneously, Billy Sunday, the baseball evangelist, found his appeal fading. As early as 1915 the *Literary Digest* contrasted his revivalistic techniques with Ford's industrial methods, and of these "two methods of conversion" found the work ethic preferable to the modified doctrine of grace that Sunday offered. Increasingly, Americans viewed business leaders as the proper channels for Christianity, and many ministers protested that the new American "conception of God is that he is a sort of Magnified Rotarian."[3]

When Bruce Barton, preacher's son and advertising man, wrote the best-selling *The Man That Nobody Knows,* Americans were ready to agree that if Christ were to return he would transform twelve men into the best management team on earth and change the world through proper business methods. If Americans sought a living example of such a commercial prophet, they found Henry Ford declaring that "The Sermon on the Mount" was the credo of his organization. The Five Dollar Day and the Model T offered an industrial method which allowed "the meek to inherit the earth." Tributes to Ford began to take on a special tone; he had reached a new apotheosis as a spiritual leader who distributed material benefits. After he announced a spectacular price cut of over $100 per car to his 1920 customers, one newspaper eulogized: "Your life, your character, and your achievements should be an inspiration. . . . plain, simple, good-hearted, just, generous, Henry Ford! The American people love such characters as you. Men like you are a blessing to the world."[4]

Ford's blessing had taken the form of a constantly lowering price on his automobiles, cut from over $900 in 1909 to $360 in 1920, despite his continuing inability to make cars fast enough to meet demand. The rush of cars had transformed the United States in a single generation. When the Lynd's made their famous study of a typical American city,[5] they found virtually every institution had been reshaped by the automobile, and Americans were acutely aware of the change.

In 1900 the first car appeared in Middletown; by 1923 there were 6,221, one for every 6.1 citizens. As in the rest of the nation, over 40% of these were Fords. Perhaps even more important, nearly all were made on assembly lines using the techniques Ford had developed, and many of those who could purchase automobiles were themselves employed in related industries. By the end of the 1920's, automotive manufacturers used 20% of the nation's steel, 80% of its rubber, and 75% of its plate glass, while also creating a whole range of subsidiaries and service facilities.

In addition to transforming the world of production, the automobile altered domestic life. Families no longer felt it necessary to live near their work or close to the center of town. But as a result, family members were more likely to spend time away from home and eat together less regularly. On Sunday, instead of attending church, many chose to visit recreation areas or state parks. The rural school largely disappeared, supplanted by larger facilities whose students arrived in buses. In the evening union organizers found it difficult to fill their meetings, because workers were out for a spin. The auto had such high priority and prestige that to own one many families sacrificed buying new clothing or did not install indoor plumbing.

Perhaps youth enjoyed the car the most. "On the Old Back Seat of the Henry Ford/They Didn't Mind the Rumble of the Old Buck Board." Or in the lyrics of "That Wonderful Ford":

> Oh gee, I am so happy
> I don't know what to do
> All night long I've been dreaming
> I was automobiling
> With a sweet little girlie too.

With such delights, the author concluded, "All your troubles are bubbles."[6]

Enraptured with Ford's car, Americans were willing to grant him broad powers to change other aspects of their lives. When Ford proposed to lease and complete the Muscle Shoals project, a series of dams on the Tennessee River, national support immediately emerged. The American Federation of Labor endorsed the plan in its 1922 convention, and farmers were ecstatic about the cheap fertilizers Ford promised to produce with the electricity. The South received the plan warmly, with the *Memphis Commercial-Appeal* and *Birmingham Age-Herald* leading a chorus that supported Southern congressmen. The *Literary Digest* dwelt on the wonderful effects of a project that would provide cheap fertilizer and electricity to an impoverished Appalachia, and newspapers as distant as the *Fargo Courier News* and the *Brooklyn Eagle* seconded these praises.

*The Illustrated World* compared the project to the conquests of Caesar, Alexander, and Napoleon. In the Tennessee Valley, they predicted, Ford will cross the borderland into a new realm of endeavor. Henry Ford, with Thomas A. Edison, will inaugurate—for the common folk of America—the Hydro-Electric-Chemical Age. At Muscle Shoals we will witness the culmination of centuries of patient research into the mysteries of Nature.[7]

Thus Ford's proposal had a millennial aspect. The introduction of electricity and assembly line factories in Tennessee would usher in a new age for the common man based on the scientific conquest of Nature.

With such notions in the air, land speculation spurted and a brass band greeted Ford and Edison when they arrived to tour the site. After their visit, letters poured into Dearborn supporting the Muscle Shoals bid. But not everyone rushed to celebrate the Hydro-Electric-Chemical Age. The *Nation* declared against the plan because the price was rather low, Henry Ford would clearly not live the hundred years of the proposed lease, and the rental would be a bad precedent. The magazine did not suspect Ford's intentions, however, until a later issue, when it declared that "There is no limit to Ford's daring" or to "his contempt for the puny laws that bind lesser men." Many bankers attacked the Muscle Shoals bid because Ford suggested the government should not borrow money to pay for the completion of the dams, but instead should issue money backed by the potential value of the dam itself. This "fiat money" was generally denounced in financial circles, along with Ford's proposal to pay for the rental of the completed facility through a sinking fund that would last a hundred years.

Similar arguments were advanced by Senator Norris in the United States Congress, despite a resolution from his own state legislature asking him to change his stand. The House of Representatives had already passed the proposal by a wide margin, but Norris shelved it, and all hope of passage ended.[8]

Many wondered, however, if Ford had any interest in Muscle Shoals itself, or whether he was using it for publicity in a run for the presidency. William Harding, easily elected, had proved a popular president and was still untouched by the hidden Teapot Dome scandal, which would not emerge until after his death. Yet when *Collier's Weekly* conducted a presidential poll during the summer of 1923, Ford defeated Harding 88,865 to 51,000. However accurate the poll, the size of Ford's victory is impressive, especially considering that he was never an announced candidate, that the poll was taken over a year before the conventions, and that Harding was a popular incumbent. Ford's support was neither regional nor rural. He had clear pluralities in all but six states and lost to Harding only in New York and Connecticut, the latter by a narrow margin. But Ford won handily in nearby Massachusetts and Pennsylvania. Overall the poll demonstrated Ford's national support.

Democratic leaders had other ideas, however; among 2,000 polled by *Literary Digest,* McAdoo was first with 706 votes; Ford, second with 231; and Oscar Underwood, third with 204. The difference between popular and professional opinion is a reminder that Ford was a maverick who had not clearly identified himself with either party. An outsider, his popularity stemmed from sources that ultimately transcended politics.

Naturally, some treated Ford's candidacy humorously. *Forum* suggested that he might put conveyor belts in the White House and reduce his cabinet to a cost accounting bureau. Cartoonists were also drawn to the possibility of Ford's campaign, depicting him offering a lift in his Model T to a Democratic party whose car was a wreck, or showing a Ford in armor, his Flivver careening toward other contenders in a jousting match for the nomination. But by the latter part of 1923, few thought Ford should be treated lightly. The *New Republic* took his candidacy seriously by July, arguing that he was better suited to the cabinet, since he had obvious shortcomings, while other journals speculated that perhaps the very unpredictable and unsafe aspect of his candidacy attracted the American voter.[9]

Some newspapers reported that the completion of Muscle Shoals was a plank in Ford's campaign platform, along with the abolition of the gold standard, construction of a St. Lawrence shipping canal, and creation of factories in Mexico, "to pacify it with quantity production of cheap automobiles and cheap tractors." What may have begun as an economic proposal for Muscle Shoals became part of a national attraction to Ford as a political figure.

When Ford attacked the Secretary of War, John Weeks, many assumed it was the opening shot in a campaign for the White House.[10] But Ford did not follow up this fusilade, and considerable uncertainty remained about his intentions. In Dearborn, a Henry-Ford-for-president Club had been formed in May 1922. Members told the press that the auto maker had not encouraged them, but neither had he tried to stop them. The club sought support among the seven thousand Ford dealers, and by February of 1923 had established a hundred and fifty local clubs. Thus a grass roots apparatus was available, while Ford also owned a newspaper, the *Dearborn Independent*. As an extra, Mr. Hearst inclined towards him, which along with Ford's resources ensured that a major campaign could be launched overnight.

Small wonder then that many assumed he would soon be an announced candidate. New York state farmers sent him petitions with such slogans as, "Come and lead us out," "No more politicians, lawyers or generals for us," and "You have ginger, gumption, and guts."[11] In Ford they saw relief from the agricultural depression that had gripped the country since the end of the war, not only because of his farm upbringing and his serviceable car and tractor, but also because he promised to provide inexpensive fertilizer through a nitrogen fixation process at Muscle Shoals.

Ford was associated in the public mind with the wonders of invention. He built a home adjoining Edison's in Florida, and they often appeared together, camping, at Muscle Shoals, or visiting each other at their work. Neither seemed bent upon making money. Edison, a notoriously poor businessman, had forgotten to take out an international patent on his movie projector, had sold copying patents to Mr. A. B. Dick for $500, and had received little for his invention of the electric light. Ford's voluntary rebates and wage hikes similarly showed an indifference to mere moneymaking that endeared him to many Americans. Together, the two men stood for a better life through practical science, bringing transportation, light, and entertainment to the millions.

Yet unlike Edison, Ford was a shrewd businessman. The most striking example of his acumen came in the brief recession of 1921. He had just bought out his remaining stockholders for about $100,000,000, business was poor, and rumors spread that he would be forced to borrow money from Wall Street. In sympathy many Americans wrote, offering to loan him small amounts. Business was so bad during January that he closed down the plant. Then he reopened only the assembly line, manufacturing all his spare parts into cars and forcing them on his dealers, who in turn had to sell them or borrow locally. By displacing his problem to his dealers, Ford kept the bankers out and paid his former stockholders. Surprisingly, few criticized him for treating his dealers in this way; most were impressed and amused by the skill which Ford evinced in escaping what seemed a Wall Street trap.

Ford's image was strengthened by the widespread belief that he had returned all his war profits to the government. Although he had announced he would not take a penny in profits on war production,

Ford never refunded anything to the government, largely because the federal audit of his books took so long.[12] By 1923 when it had been completed, Ford was embroiled in the Muscle Shoals controversy and in no mood to give millions of dollars to the government. The public knew nothing of these complications and believed he had not profited on the carnage of war.

Consequently, when Ford charged that wars were caused by profiteers, his position appeared impeccable. Furthermore, his opposition to the gold standard and bankers seemed to arise from personal experiences. Ford had just escaped the hands of the bankers in his own business crisis of 1921, and he seemed to be battling with them again over Muscle Shoals. He also knew how Edison had been defrauded of his rightful profits by wily financiers. To the public mind, then, Ford did not merely have a *position* on the gold standard and bankers, he had experienced trouble at their hands. Furthermore, when Ford called bankers and Jews parasites, he struck a responsive note with the American public, although in the aftermath of Hitler's atrocities, it is hard to view Ford's anti-Semitic campaign in the *Dearborn Independent* impartially, much less sympathetically. In May 1920, the *Independent* editorialized against "The International Jew: The World's Problem," and subsequent issues blamed Jews for strikes, wars, and the invention of economics! (Marx and Ricardo were Jewish.)

In 1923 most Americans did not find these absurdities dangerous, but shared them. In an age when the Ku Klux Klan reached its greatest strength, Ford's anti-Semitism was appealing. It was an era of suspicion and fear of Bolshevism, the time of the "Red Scare" and the Palmer raids. Intolerance extended to foreign social customs as well, while drinking fell under prohibition in a campaign largely supported by white Protestants and middle-class Americans and directed against immigrants. In fact, as with the Mt. Clemens trial, Ford rose in the popular estimation because of what now appear to be faults. At a time of strong isolationism, his ignorance of foreign affairs seemed unimportant. In a society where Calvin Coolidge would soon gain fame for the quip that "The business of America is business," Ford's industrial background seemed appropriate. Faults in historical retrospect were virtues at the time. Ford's very commonness, which the *Nation* decried, was the key to his appeal.

His narrowness, ignorance of history, prejudice, and "crack-brained" ideas, such as "fiat money," when perceived by his contemporaries, became persistence, simplicity, insight, and genius. His faults were theirs. Criticism of Ford they took as criticism of themselves, and he became a Moses, Napoleon, Caesar, and Alexander who would lead them to a promised land symbolized by Muscle Shoals and already partially revealed by the wonders of the electric light and the Tin Lizzie. He would "inaugurate—for the common folk of America—the Hydro-Electric-Chemical Age."

The coalescence of factors which thrust Ford into the presidential race ultimately created a messianic figure. Semireligious imagery began to cluster about him. Even the usually critical *Forum* fell partially under the spell, printing a poem which sums up the mixture of practicality and utopianism Ford represented.[13]

### To Henry Ford

Have you ever read a poem, Henry Ford?
Perhaps you will notice this one about you.

How would it be to choose for President
The richest and simplest man alive
Whose only gospel is the gospel of work,
And whose major faith is faith in Henry Ford?
That eye, that quick shrewd eye, to watch a country!

We laughed at you, your road-louse, your Lizzie
Laughed at your ship of peace in time of war
Called you to witness, made a fool of you,
Mocked you to death and went about our business;
But now we think of you for President

Witter Bynner, the author, has already introduced a covert reference to Christ, who was also "mocked to death" and who called for peace in time of war. He then recalls,

I met you for a moment, during the war,
A little gray man with an honest eye,
And on the tip of your nose—there at the very tip,
I see it still—was a bruise, a scab, a token.
You spoke of it yourself. "It came," you said,
"From studying a tractor wheel too close."

> Would you knock your nose again, as President?
> Or would you enter through the eye of a needle,
> Pulling the country after you like a thread,
> Into a heaven made of smoke and brick,
> With sweat for crowns and dinner pails for wings,
> And living wages from the God of things?

Bynner alludes to Christ's words that it would be as difficult for a rich man to enter heaven as for a camel to pass through the eye of a needle, compounding the difficulty with images of the country as a thread and dinner pails as wings to show how unlikely a deliverance Ford offered. His heaven would be "made of smoke and brick," perhaps a covert reference to Hades. But whatever control one grants this poet, he clearly takes Ford seriously as a possible secular messiah, whose gospel of work may provide living wages from the "God of things."

A less self-conscious attitude toward Ford composed of the same elements was Rev. William Stidger's *Henry Ford: The Man and His Motives* (1923), which was meant to demonstrate Ford's presidential stature.[14] Stidger was Ford's personal friend, and his book was screened before publication. Despite this precaution, however, there was a power-ful ambivalence to Ford's River Rouge Plant latent in Stidger's imagery despite his conscious intentions. After exulting in the "miracle" and "romance" of the factory, which could turn raw materials into cars in *three* days, Stidger descends from the "high place" where he has been surveying the Plant

> to the foundries where great molten kettles of white-hot iron were swinging on great run-ways propelled by huge black men from the sunny south; men, who in the blare and glare of splashing, simmering, smoldering iron, open furnaces with streams of molten, running iron, men who look like figures *from some grim Rembrandt picture.*
>
> That journey from the top of that bridge down the elevator into the furnace room of the blast furnace, through the power plants, into the foundry reminded me of a journey that *Dante* once took with a certain guide who showed him exactly the same kind of things that Mr. Smith showed to me from that high height and throughout the works on that winter's day [emphasis added].

Stidger's references to "some grim Rembrandt" and to Dante's descent into the Inferno suggest that the foundry was hell and its black workers damned. Unconsciously Stidger recognized the import of what he saw, recording it in images which ran counter to his intentions.

Nor did Dante's *Divine Comedy* disappear from Stidger's thoughts. The image of the inferno was retained and expressed in an unintentional parody of the most famous line of that poem, as Stidger gazed about, looking for a suitable inscription. "I looked at a sign on the furnace down in the furnace room which read: 'Henry Ford—1917–1920/Began Operation, May 17th, 1920/11:58 A.M.'" Instead of the famous admonition to abandon all hope, Ford begins all work for those who enter here! Stidger preserves the pattern of Dante's work by looking for a sign which will explain the significance of the scene; the juxtaposition is a covert recognition of the hellish aspects of a scene he strives to love and admire.

In the Power Plant Stidger's language again records a mixture of conscious observation and covert antipathy.

Then we went to the power plant. *There is none such in the world.* They burn gas which they manufacture from their own coal, a by-product of coke making; they burn coal tar; they burn pulverized coal so fine that ninety-five percent of it can go through a quarter-inch screen.

Power! Power! Power! That is the source of the romance of the River Rouge Plant, so it was well to see whence it came.

There is a curious juxtaposition here of factual material and imagistic language, of mechanical description and romantic ecstasy, Stidger passes directly from an account of the materials burned in the furnace to an exultant repetition of the word "Power," followed by the assertion that this power is the source of romance. But on a much deeper level, he is clearly antipathetic to the power which attracts him. The earlier references to a "high place" combined with other Biblical imagery in his work reminds us that Stidger, like most Americans, was steeped in Christianity. The high place of most prominence in the New Testament is that Satan led Christ to, offering him the Kingdoms of the world. Similarly, Ford has been given dominion over a vast industrial empire, and he is explicitly compared to Christ.

As Stidger looks down from the tops of the blast furnaces, his guide, Mr. Smith, asserts:

those human beings are the climax of a miracle—that other miracle which you as a minister ought to know about. . . . I mean the miracle of the loaves and the fishes. Those mountains of raw materials have not only been transformed into tractors but into food for human beings, only these particular "loaves and fishes" will feed a hundred thousand people today. . . .

Here is Weber's romance of numbers, the American love of bigness that was the final product of the Protestant Ethic once it had been stripped of its religious vesture. Sheer size and the quantity of good works become the tests of a man's moral worth, and the miraculous took on a numerical coefficient.

The numbers are so intoxicating that Stidger avers what cannot be literally true—that the iron ore and other raw materials will feed men. And though nothing done in the factory can lead directly to the literal production of men, that is also asserted: "Therein lies the great miracle and the great romance! The ore piles are transformed into human bodies and human food and human happiness. That is the real romance of the River Rouge!" Yet while consciously Stidger may assert this absurdity, on another level, in his imagery, he locates another response to the factory and its raw materials: they are "elemental as the crater of a volcano into the mouth of which I have looked down in Java." The inferno Ford has prepared is latently as explosive as a volcano. The "miracle" of producing food and men is in fact a fiery consummation. Implicitly Ford has turned stone into bread, succumbing to the temptation of Christ.

Thus despite his attempt to propagandize for Ford, Stidger expressed ambivalent feelings towards industrial power. His meticulous descriptions are coupled with exultant and triumphant rhetoric which is suddenly punctured, albeit unconsciously, by images which suggest the opposite of the surface meaning. Stidger's failure to integrate his imagery, rhetoric, and description indicates the ambivalence which lurks beneath his apparent meaning.

The uneasy mixture of Christian imagery and Ford's industry was characteristic not only of a magazine poem in *Forum* or a popular study of Ford. Many Americans perceived Ford in Biblical terms, as in a petition which stated, "You are the Moses for 80% of us," which arrived in support of the Muscle Shoals project. Ford thus became the leader of an embattled people who were struggling to reach a promised industrial utopia, and some of his workers sang "A Thanksgiving Hymn to be sung to the tune of 'Onward Christian Soldiers,'" written by Mrs. Jessie Bilodeau, an employee at Ford Factory.[15]

## HENRY FORD—A FAITHFUL SHEPHERD

### I

HENRY FORD is kingly, powerful and kind,
    For he is a servant of our loving GOD;
He is serving graciously with all those who plod
    For the need and welfare of GOD's lambs—mankind.

(Chorus)
HENRY FORD IS KINGLY, POWERFUL AND KIND:
HE IS SERVING GRACIOUSLY ALL GOD'S LAMBS—MANKIND.

### II

Onward faithful workers, toil with HENRY FORD,—
    Toil is Heav'n-sent, choose it and its honors claim;
Let us laud FORD eagerly, hearts and souls aflame,
    He is our great work-chief, sent us from the LORD.

### III

Join in honest praises for this king 'mong men,—
    Heed his every precept while we labor here;
Render loyal service, too, there is naught to fear—
    He will smooth life's troubled way with both deeds and pen.

### IV

Thanks to GOD in Heaven for our HENRY FORD!
    There are those who scorn him but we know him best,—
Do the square thing, workers, and he'll do the rest;
    Tho he may not claim it, he's a servant of the LORD.

Those who sang these words naturally recalled the original verses as well;
the combination of the two with the march time of the music could
only reenforce the explicit meaning. Henry Ford is a secular messiah,
"kingly, powerful, and kind," "a servant of the Lord" who has been sent
to lead "God's lambs," mankind, in the work/battle to purify the world
and enter a "promised land." One owes him a blind obedience and "loyal
service," "and he'll do the rest." Underpinning this message is the repeated
rhyme Ford/Lord emphasizing their identity. The hymn is an explicit

avowal of faith uncomplicated by Bynner's doubts or Stidger's unconscious recognitions.

Nationally, such uncompromising faith was probably extreme, but the identity Ford/Lord did recur in the Lizzie label, the antecedent of the present bumper sticker. These apothegms and rhymes reached their height in the 1920's. Like the earlier Ford joke, many sought to present the Model T as the car of the common man, or to make light of its importance in humorous contempt: "Another fossil," "Relic of a bygone day," "Haywire Bound," and the thrifty "Don't laugh, I'm paid for." As B. A. Botkin concluded "most of the Ford jokes originated in the self-consciousness of the Ford owner, out of the need of forestalling or averting criticism."[16] Sensing their own poverty compared to the owners of Pierce-Arrows and in a sense their social insignificance, Ford owners displaced their inferiority to the automobile, but in defiant humor. Symptomatically, a whole class of Lizzie labels began with "Don't laugh . . ."

Simultaneously, however, in compensation Ford himself was raised to a new level of cultural significance. As a messianic industrialist, he provided the ultimate answer to the rich, leading his customers to a better life. The labels recognized that every aspect of American life had been touched by the car, from the life cycle and the home to popular amusements and education. And some of them recognized the same identity between Ford and Lord which had intrigued Bynner, disturbed Stidger, and inspired the Ford hymn. Beyond the defensiveness and the celebrations of the joys afforded by the rumble seat, many of the Lizzie labels reflected a sense of Ford's impact on the American scene. Some were mock apocalyptic: "Abandon hope, all ye who enter here," "In God we trust," and "No return tickets sold." Others explicitly recognized that Ford had in a sense replaced God: "The Lord giveth and the Ford taketh away" and "Sunday is no longer the Lord's day, it is the Ford's day."

The Lizzie labels mirror the American awareness of Ford's impact on their lives. So long as he seemed to fulfill the desires of those caught within an industrial system, ensuring their well-being, and so long as he seemed to affirm the pioneer tradition through industry, he would serve as a messianic figure. To buy his Model T was to participate in his probe of the secrets of the universe at Muscle Shoals. To support him for the presidency was to affirm the march of progress, the harmony of nature and technology, and the possibility of utopia.

Ford refused the presidency, declaring he could do more where he was. Harding's sudden death sealed this decision, for Calvin Coolidge's image was similar to Ford's. None questioned Coolidge's honesty or integrity; indeed, he seemed to exemplify old-fashioned Yankee virtue, caution, and parsimony. He was dubbed "silent Cal" for an allegedly taciturn nature. The Teapot Dome scandal did not become associated with him, and he emerged as a powerful candidate for reelection. Furthermore, his belief that government should do as little as possible assured industrialists like Ford a free rein.

In December of 1923, shortly after a private meeting with the new president, Ford announced his support for Coolidge amid speculation that in return he would receive the rights to Muscle Shoals, although this never happened. So the Ford presidential boom ended. During it a consensus had been achieved about the nature of Ford's abilities and what he represented, as supporters and detractors shared certain beliefs about his nature. He might be interpreted according to various standards. For example, both the *Nation* and many rural newspapers agreed that Ford was essentially a typical shop foreman but differed radically in their interpretation of this "fact." To the *Nation* it signified Ford's unfitness for public office; to rural editors it was his claim to the presidency. His typicality was symbolic.

A psychological portrait was fixed and sketched in such books as *Famous Leaders of Industry* (1920), *Twenty-One Americans* (1921), *Contemporary Immortals* (1927), *The Story of Famous Fortunes* (1931), and *The Quick and the Dead* (1931). Each depicted a humane man, rising from humble origins, struggling through middle life to build the Model T. Ford was intelligent, but hard work rather than genius accounted for his success. Deemphasizing the Peace Ship, omitting the Mt. Clemens trial, "no one could better represent this time and the United States than Henry Ford."

In spite of his new ideas, drawn from things outside his business, which have mixed him up and made him make mistakes, the story of Ford's life still shows him as he is—the farmer's son turned mechanic, shrewd, patient, suspicious, and calculating, putting his trust in action, and driven on without rest by a single idea which has lifted him from a position of need to a position of titanic power.[17]

In the sixty years since Ford's birth, the United States had achieved its own titanic power, although still rhetorically committed to the individualism which had characterized the largely agricultural and rural republic. Ford personified this power and an individualism apparently adequate to create and control it. He was "the farmer's son turned mechanic." His rural qualities explained both him and the nation's success. The implicit messianic nature of Ford's role would not become explicit again until the identification between him and the nation underwent stress in the closing years of the 1920's, as his own business, and then the nation's, collapsed.

Ford's percentage of the market declined during the 1920's because General Motors and others began to offer cars with numerous improvements which the Model T did not have, such as three-speed transmissions, electric starters, foot (instead of hand) brakes, and rear gas tanks. General Motors sales increased by 50%; Ford's marked time, although the Tudor sedan's price dropped each year. Dependability and service, once unusual, were now taken for granted, and automobiles needed aesthetic appeal and convenience as well. Annual style changes were introduced to suggest that rapid advances in design were made each year, and credit buying grew in popularity, making it possible for many to purchase more expensive models.

In the crisis Ford initially refused to allow the Lizzie to be changed, believing that his public would return. He organized pep talks, abolished dealership territories, increased the number of dealers, cut back on clerical personnel, slashed prices, and did everything but change the car's design. But by May 26, 1927, he recognized that the Model T's days were over, announcing his decision to stop making it as the 15,000,000th Lizzie rolled off the assembly line.

Public reaction was immediate. Tremendous interest developed in the new cars Ford might make, but an equally strong nostalgia sprang up over the demise of the Model T. The *Nation* sadly noted its passing and reflected that people stopped buying the car when "They were not so interested in going anywhere as they were in being seen going somewhere." The car was spoken of as though it had been a person. The Model T "was sturdy, strong, and brave," and it had acquired the affectionate nickname "Tin Lizzie." It was at once a symbol of the forces changing society and of a simpler existence. It embodied two contradictory impulses: to leave the inner city and return to the land, and to change American life through the use of technology—to simplify, paradoxically, through the machine.

Affection for the car included Ford. As the *Nation* noted in a second article,

> During the last quarter century machines have been carried to the farthest village in the country. Telephones, the telegraph, mechanical devices. . . . Yet what man thinks tenderly of his cream separator? And who looks on a telephone except with impatience and contumely? Henry Ford . . . alone won the hearts of his customers. . . .[18]

Ford was not merely selling a product. Just as his car was a symbol unifying contradictory impulses, Ford himself seemed to reconcile the impulses towards the garden and the machine. Likewise his Five Dollar Day seemed to demonstrate that free enterprise led directly to social welfare, and to show that vast personal fortune need not impair the chances of others on the ladder of success.

It was a crisis of faith. The Model T was an American icon which had to be replaced. Nostalgia for the old car was coupled with an intense national interest in its successor. The king was dead—a new king as worthy must be found. The nature of this event emerges when it is viewed in religious terms. A more recent commentator had this to say about "the cult of the sacred automobile."

> One need merely visit the annual automobile show to realize that it is a highly ritualized religious performance. The colors, the lights, the music, the awe of the worshippers, the presence of the temple priestesses (fashion models), the pomp and splendor, the lavish waste of money, the thronging crowd—all these would represent in any other culture a clearly liturgical service. . . . The cult of the sacred car has its adepts and initiati. No gnostic more eagerly awaited a revelation from an oracle than does an automobile worshipper await the first rumors about the new models. It is at this time of the annual seasonal cycle that the high priests of the cult—the auto dealers—take on a new importance as an anxious public eagerly expects the coming of a new form of salvation.[19]

Andrew Greeley describes a much later, formalized expression of emotions which the demise of the Model T brought to a height. This was not the end of a seasonal cycle. There had been but one Ford in the public mind—or rather fifteen million identical Fords, a democratic dispersal of a sacred object which reconciled the tensions and oppositions in life. And now it was gone, while in secrecy Ford worked alone.

Even the dealers knew nothing. Growing restless, some even traveled to
Detroit in hopes of finding out when delivery might begin.

A product had not been discontinued; "she" had died, and with her
a store of folk humor and stories. Competitors, Chevrolet especially,
made tremendous gains, but could hardly produce in large enough
quantities to fill the void. Thousands deferred purchase of a new car
to see what Ford would unveil. Almost half a million Americans made
payments on the unknown car without knowing its price or description.
Here was faith indeed.

By August 1927 the new car had been created, although it was not
yet ready for production. Nearly all of the five thousand parts were
entirely new. Ford had spared no expense, cut no corners, but had declared craftsmanship alone was important. He told the public, in effect,
that his part would be properly played, that the new car would not be
made for profit, but for the public welfare. Mechanical perfection was
paramount.

During the next three months supposed descriptions and pictures
of the new Ford were front page news. Dealers continued to ask for
information. Finally the car appeared on December 2, and across the
nation showrooms were besieged. In New York crowds began gathering
outside showrooms at 3 A.M. By 9:00 police were called out to keep
order, as all the surrounding streets were jammed. Despite a cold rain,
200,000 New Yorkers managed to see the Model A, 15,000 making
immediate downpayments without a test drive. In Detroit "Ten
thousand persons pushed, shoved, and jostled to get into Convention
Hall at 10 A.M., "including people from all walks of life." In New
Orleans 23 people saw the car every minute, including "businessmen,
St. Bernard and Jefferson truck farmers, housewives, jellybeans and
flappers." In Newark latecomers tried to see the Ford with a ladder,
and in Pittsburgh a huge crowd caused a near riot at an assembly plant.
In the first day, over 10,000,000 Americans fought to see the New Ford.

Why should a new automobile be called "The Greatest Show on
Earth"?[20] Why did ordinary citizens stay up all night for a glimpse of
its black exterior? Such enthusiasm cannot be based on aesthetics or
curiosity alone. Some had an economic interest, since a minor recession
had been partially attributed to Ford's shutdown, and thousands had
been jobless for nearly a year. Yet these were not artists, bankers, or
the jobless who lined the streets.

The new car did not raise aesthetic, economic, or humorous questions,
but ultimately posed the problem of regeneration. Could Ford make

another car as inexpensive and durable as the first one? Shorn of many
key executives who had gone to his competitors, could his corporation
renew itself? Americans believed in Henry Ford. They had tried to
regenerate America through prohibition, the exclusion of aliens, and
the elevation of business to a secular religion. They had compared
Ford to Moses, Napoleon, Caesar, and even Christ, making him their
agent of salvation. In 1923 millions had believed he might lead them
into a new era, symbolized by Muscle Shoals. Now he had to save himself. If he could, it would be a victory for the embattled farmer mired
in continuing rural depression, a triumph of common sense and hard
work over the forces of the marketplace. Put more abstractly, the birth
of the Model A was an affirmation that traditional American values
could survive in the industrial world. Like the Model T, which had
embodied contradictory impulses, the New Ford testified to the survival
of agrarian simplicity in a new technological form.

Years earlier Henry Adams had suppressed his impulse to worship
the dynamo.[21] Now the appearance of a new machine was greeted with
a spontaneous civic enthusiasm and a kind of secular worship. But
it was to be the last great public outpouring on Ford's behalf. In the
coming depression crowds would also gather, but they would be neither
spontaneous nor enthusiastic. They would not be concerned with the
welfare of a machine, but with their own personal welfare. Ford, who
had been leader and hero, to many would soon seem an enemy.

# CHAPTER THREE

# BREAD AND BULLETS

Ford, confidant of four previous presidents, seldom went to the White House during Roosevelt's administrations. The interests of large business and government no longer seemed identical as the New Deal emphasized regulation of the economy. With thirteen million unemployed, it was not in Roosevelt's interest to be identified too closely with the rich. Where before a ladder of success had seemed to extend from the worker to the wealth of his employer, a gulf now opened between them. As a widening circle of debt spread through society, leaving many destitute, Henry Ford's life did not seem a plausible model for the average American. His wealth, once a tribute to the free enterprise system, to some became its indictment.

In each decade Ford reflected the relative cohesion of his society. If the 1920's had been a period of broad consensus based on an expansive economy, when political dissent was ignored, the 1930's were marked by increasing political polarization and ideological clash that persisted so long as the economy remained sluggish. As the Depression wore on, Ford's messianic image would be challenged and transformed until three figures emerged expressing different political persuasions.

Ford's image, however, did not break down as rapidly as the economy, but over two years weakened and disintegrated as it became clear that he, like other American business leaders, was unable to reverse the economic contraction. After the stock market crash in 1929, Ford met with President Hoover and announced the Seven Dollar Day, promising a rapid recovery. But such high wages proved unrealistic and had to be discontinued, as yearly income in the automotive and related industries fell from $1,638 to $1,035 in the following four years. Not only had wages plummeted, but many were not employed; those who were suffered under relentless speed-ups. Magazine articles about Ford also plummeted to less than half the volume of pre-Depression years.

A further index of the public's loss of enthusiasm for Ford is the contrast between reviews of his *My Life and Work* (1922) and *Moving Forward* (1930). The first had been hailed as a handbook to success; the second was received with doubts and some ambivalence. A typical reviewer summarized, "The book may be accepted as an authoritative exposition of Ford theory and practice—the untempered, marvelously egoistic expression of a man of genius who had better be listened to even when he appears to be talking self-contradictory nonsense." Less charitably, another found "Mr. Ford in the mantle of a philosopher . . . a pathetic and transient figure." While most credited Ford with "factory wisdom" it no longer carried over from industry to other matters. Reviewers tended to escape from analyzing the social consequences of Ford's ideas by splitting him into a practical industrialist and a nonsensical philosopher. To dismiss his ideas as foolishness, however, did not prevent them from being implemented. Ford's belief that "to make employment regular is to invite industrial decay," for example, was not merely an amusing vagary, but found expression in layoffs and irregular work for thousands. Reviewers tended to ignore this actuality, however.[1]

They were confronted more directly with possible implications of Ford's work in Aldous Huxley's *Brave New World.* Reviewers read of a dystopia whose crosses had been converted to T's and whose citizens swore in the name of Ford. They had no children; babies were produced in biological factories using assembly line techniques, and they were brought up as standardized parts, according to the methods of "Our Ford." Even "folk wisdom" referred to him: "Ford's in his flivver and all's right with the world." Yet neither the *Nation, New Republic, New Statesman,* nor *Forum* mentioned that Huxley's satire dealt with Ford; no major magazine paid more than passing notice. It appeared to be "merely silly."[2]

Jonathan Leonard's popular biography, *The Tragedy of Henry Ford* (1932), attempted to confront the issue of Ford's impact on the quality of life, but retreated into nostalgia. Leonard announced in his opening chapter that he had intended to write "in a fine fury of indignation."

He had seen the Ford factory, the workmen with their dull eyes, their rapid dull hands, obeying their mechanical drill masters as slavishly as if they were valve stems. . . . He had heard about Ford's cruelty, his insensitivity, his intolerance, his hatred. . . . He had observed his maniacal attacks on the Jews.

In short, after knowing several auto workers, "He had felt the heat of that hatred toward Ford and all his works which had seared the edges of nearly every human spirit in Detroit." But Leonard was unable to stick to this opening image. He also discovered an elderly Ford surrounded by children, straggling across open fields, deploying around a bush, until a song sparrow darted from its nest to "flutter on the ground with the pretense of a broken wing. Across the mobile features of Henry Ford" he saw "an expression of sympathy."

Leonard's book reconciled the cruel master of industry and the kindly birdwatcher by presenting Ford as a "pathetic, wandering man." By emphasizing this senile figure Leonard escaped his problem. Once Ford was divested of strength and intellectual coherence there was no need to question the social implications of his industrial power. Thus the book closed with the image of Ford purchasing and renovating the historic Wayside Inn, while demanding that the highway which passed nearby be moved because it interrupted his reverie. After banishing cars, he would be free to dream over the old post road, to imagine "a hundred years of covered wagons filled with Yankee women and children, off to people the West."[3] The Ford who was a vigorous presidential candidate six years earlier, who supervised the invention of the Model A, and who would battle the New Deal's National Recovery Administration (NRA) was divested of strength and made a senile antiquarian. Although he had led the nation toward an industrial utopia, Americans could now see Ford primarily in terms of the past. An anachronism, he was less frequently sought out for his forecasts. By 1932 his symbolic utility had waned. His life momentarily seemed as much a relic of the past as the Wayside Inn.

Say, I'm goin' to Detroit, I'm gonna get myself a job
I'm tired of layin' round here workin' on this starvation farm
Say, I'm goin' to get me a job now, workin' in Mr. Ford's place
Say, that woman told me last night, "Say you cannot even stand Mr.
Ford's ways."[4]

If the popular magazines began to ignore Ford, many workers did not have that luxury. Farmers mired in the continuing rural depression that had begun after World War I were forced off the family farm to Detroit, sometimes only for the winter, often permanently. Black sharecroppers were particularly drawn to Detroit, after Ford opened employment to them in 1914 and sent recruiters South. The lyrics above were part of a blues tradition dealing with the migration North. Thousands of Black Americans worked at Ford plants in St. Louis, Chicago, Detroit, and other cities, lured by the Five Dollar Day from the "starvation farm," only to find that "you cannot even stand Mr. Ford's ways."

Blacks and other workers objected to the monotony of the assembly line, the enforced silence, and the speed of the work. One Detroit worker, Walter Cunningham, wrote a bitter pamphlet, *J 8* as "A Chronicle of the Neglected Truth About Henry Ford and The Ford Motor Company." The title "was chosen because it signified 'lost identity.'" J 8 was the author's employee number, and he felt that "In exchange for the identity numbers and our wages we gave to the Ford Motor Company not only eight hours labor, but we also surrendered our personality, individuality, and inventive genius, if any."[5] Cunningham's complaints about the repetitive work, the speed-ups, the incredibly short rest and eating periods, and the constant surveillance of the Ford Service Department were common among workers. They could not dismiss these daily hardships by simply ignoring them as the magazines did, or by viewing Ford as an old man, as Leonard had done in his biography.

Joining this groundswell of opposition were increasing numbers of intellectuals, who began to identify with the workers. Edmund Wilson, for example, composed an article in English dialect, purporting to be an immigrant mechanic's reaction to Ford's plant. He said, "It's worse than the army, I tell ye—ye're badgered and victimized all the time . . . at Ford's ye never know where ye're at," and concluded, "A man checks 'is brains and 'is freedom at the door when he goes to work at Ford's." Intellectuals such as Wilson began to identify with working people, and to attack the industrial system. As Richard Pells concluded in *Radical Visions and American Dreams,* "In every area of thought . . . capitalism was identified as a threat to creativity and an implacable opponent of cultural revolution, while socialism was seen as the sole protector of art and science in the twentieth century."[6] The alienation and expatriation of American artists common in the 1920's gave way to an intense search for identification with laboring people and the hope that a new community might be forged linking the interests of the artist with the proletariat.

However, the working class they sought was far less ready to embrace revolution than they were, and only a series of jarring strikes and economic crises would move workers to unionize. One of the more important of these events was the "Dearborn Massacre," a march of Ford workers organized by the Detroit Unemployed Councils and the Automobile Workers' Union. In March 1932 several thousand men and women gathered on a blustery cold day. None were armed, and their leaders called for an orderly, nonviolent protest as they demanded payment of 50% of full wages, a slow-down of the assembly line, two fifteen-minute rest breaks daily, and abolition of the Ford spy system. While the crowd was sizable, it represented but a fraction of those who had been laid off.

Police met the marchers at the Dearborn town line and tried to turn them back verbally, but the crowd pressed forward. Accounts of what followed differ according to which side they come from, but this much is certain: after spraying them with tear gas, much of which was blown away by the wind, police retreated. Tensions increased as the police tried fire hoses and workers retaliated with stones. Ford service personnel joined the police, a shot was fired, and soon the marchers were fleeing from a barrage of small arms fire, as twenty-three were shot, four of them fatally. Investigators found most had been wounded in the back.

This disaster galvanized the workers of Detroit, who attended mass meetings to protest the killings and thronged to the angry funeral. The slain became martyrs, and across the nation intellectuals already predisposed to identify themselves with a proletariat they had just discovered could rise to their defense. Their response, however, must be seen as part of a general pattern. Three different reactions to the "Dearborn Massacre" emerged, reflecting ideological cleavages. Conservatives condemned the workers for being deluded and stirred up by a Communist leader, William Z. Foster, "ex-convict and dangerous radical, who is said to have delivered an inflammatory address at the meeting in which the demonstration was arranged." Conservatives contrasted events in Dearborn with the more orderly march led by Father

Cox in Washington, and newspapers in Los Angeles, Colorado Springs, and Philadelphia editorialized against "rioting reds" and "mob violence."[7]

Ford was a hero to many right-wing Americans intent on preserving a nineteenth-century laissez-faire economy against the encroachments of socialism. Throughout the rest of his life Ford would be their exemplar, sought as an ally by Father Couglin, Charles Lindberg, Doctor Townsend, and others who resisted the New Deal. For example, in the 1940's the Fellowship Press of Indianapolis described Ford as "the Christian patriarch of American industrialists" in their pamphlet "Henry Ford Swims the Red Sea: The Man Who Gave You the Inexpensive Motor Car Defies America's Bolsheviki." The "Christian American system of Free enterprise" which he represented was threatened by "Red elements . . . working insidiously throughout every American industry."[8]

However, the moderate majority refused to accept conspiratorial views of the "Massacre." The Detroit papers at first worried that there had been a "Communist riot," but within two days agreed that unwarranted police violence had caused the trouble. The *Detroit News,* for example, editorialized on "How Orderly Hunger March Turned into Bloody Battle." Across the country most newspapers followed this line of thought, blaming police for their poor handling of the affair. When the Ford Motor Company was discussed, the Ford Service Department was criticized, especially Harry Bennett, who ran it, but Henry Ford was often not mentioned. Just as, in 1927, the public had been willing to believe that Ford had nothing to do with the anti-Semitic attacks of his newspaper, now they were willing to absolve him of responsibility for the deaths of four workers, blaming unnamed others, poor police methods, or the unfortunate mood of the times.[9]

Ford's enormous reservoir of good will created in the 1920's would not dissipate immediately. During the following year many sympathized with him when he refused to join Roosevelt's NRA because he disapproved of governmental interference. Ford's position was especially strong, because he met every NRA guideline voluntarily. As a result the *Nation* was forced to admit that Ford's position looked better than Roosevelt's, especially when the administration tried to prevent all federal agencies from buying Ford cars. This action violated the administration's own orders, which did not require businesses to sign, but only to follow the NRA regulations to be eligible for government contracts. Ford seemed to be acting on principle; the president did not.

To many, however, Ford's principles were precisely the problem. To the *New Republic* the struggle between Ford and the president was "between rugged American individualism and a collective administration" which realized that "the automobile industry, like industry in general, is no longer in the pioneer stage." Ford's refusal to accede to liberal reform could lead to the destruction of the American system altogether. "Will the wild horses of pioneer America at last be tamed to drive in harness?" the editors asked. "If Henry Ford fights and wins," they feared, "capitalism in America will be well on its way to complete self-destruction."[10]

To those on the left such prophecies almost seemed certainties in the wake of the "Dearborn Massacre." International Pamphlets proclaimed "The End of the Ford Myth" in a widely distributed publication which began, "The Ford Myth has been washed away in blood. The legend of high wages, good conditions, [and] contented workers was riddled by the bullets which killed four unemployed workers. . . ." After a dramatic retelling of the poor conditions at Ford's plant and of the events of March 7, the pamphlet concluded with an analogy between the American situation and that of Russian workers in 1905 Petrograd: "when they asked for bread—bullets. And when they had buried their dead they had learned a lesson—to expect nothing from the capitalist class, and to prepare for working class emancipation. . . . Twelve years later . . . they smashed the whole rotten structure of capitalism. . . . So also must the workers of America answer the Ford Massacre."[11] In this vision Ford was the archetypal exploitative capitalist. He was the product of inevitable economic forces moving through history, and he would be destroyed by the massed workers of his own factory as soon as they were organized.

To conservatives, liberals, and communists Henry Ford stood as a symbol of American capitalism. But to each group, he represented far different values, ranging from rugged individualism, to anachronistic laissez-faire liberalism, to the worst form of exploitative capitalism. According to these three viewpoints, the "Dearborn Massacre" was either a heroic defense of the American system against insidious agitators, an unfortunate use of violence, or a symptom of the coming revolution.

In the middle 1930's the apocalyptic vision of Ford did not prevail;
a secular messiah does not die so easily. When the new Ford V-8 was
introduced just three weeks after the news of the "Dearborn Massacre"
almost 6,000,000 Americans rushed to see it the first day. Excitement
was moderate compared to 1927, but it persisted. Nor had nostalgia
over the Model T disappeared; many were still on the highway. Four
years later E. B. White would write his often reprinted eulogy to the
Lizzie, "Farewell, My Lovely" which appeared as both an essay and
book. In contrast to the harsh realities of the 1930's, White described
the Model T as

... the miracle God had wrought. ... As a vehicle, it was hard-working,
commonplace, heroic; and it often seemed to transmit those qualities
to the persons who rode in it. My own generation identifies it with
Youth, with its gaudy, irretrievable excitements. ...

Recalling that "the old Ford practically was the American scene,"
White threw a haze of sentimentality over the car, associating it with
halcyon days never to return. Where in 1927 it had briefly stood for
the unity of an agrarian past and an industrial future, now it appeared
a token of that lost time when "The days were golden, the nights were
dim and strange."

It sometimes nuzzled its owner; "it was like a horse, rolling the bit
on its tongue, and country people brought to it the same technique
they used with draft animals." It triumphed over the natural elements,
but was not detached from the round of the seasons. "Springtime in the
heyday of the Model T was a delirious season. Owning a car was still a
major excitement, roads were wonderful and bad. ... Boys used to veer
them off the highway into a level pasture and run wild with them, as
though they were cutting up with a girl."[12] In this bucolic vision,
the car was not an agent of change, but its victim.

The response aroused by the Model T was less a matter of thought
than of feeling, and what Leo Marx has defined as a "sentimental pastoralism" obscured the automobile's real significance. Sentimental
pastoralism is an escapist tendency expressed in many aspects of
American life, from advertisements that associate products with the
natural environment to the continuing popularity of westerns in the
media. Such phenomena "express something of the yearning for a
simpler, more harmonious style of life, an existence 'closer to nature,'

that is the psychic root of all pastoralism." "Whenever people turn away from the hard social and technological realities this obscure sentiment is likely to be at work,"[13] and one could find no more striking example than the response to Henry Ford in the 1930's.

This simple pastoralism had always been a part of Ford's appeal, along with the Algeresque aspects of his success and the utopian promise of material abundance of the assembly line. But in the 1930's when his life could no longer serve as so convenient a model of the average American life, and when the assembly line began to represent unemployment and overproduction, only the pastoral aspect of Ford's life was appealing.

The sentimental pastoralism which enveloped Ford and his car prevented Americans from understanding that the machine he had invented was one of the principle agents of change which had brought them to the collective dilemma of the 1930's. As Ortega y Gasset put it in *The Revolt of the Masses,*

The world is a civilised one, its inhabitant is not: he does not see the civilisation of the world around him, but uses it as if it were a natural force. The new man wants his motor car, and enjoys it, but he believes that it is the spontaneous fruit of an Edenic tree. In the depths of his soul he is unaware of the artificial, almost incredible, character of civilisation. . . .[14]

Because Americans typically considered their social system a kind of "natural force," they were unwilling to conceive of government regulation as anything other than a violation of the rightful order. Likewise, the unemployed worker characteristically could not rid himself of the suspicion that he was to blame for being out of work; his fundamental world view did not allow him to blame the social organization for his personal misfortune. His individualistic ideology made it impossible to accept the notion that the state was responsible for his condition.

The 1920's politician had been especially prone to promulgate the notion that society ran best with a minimum of interference, that it was in some mysterious way natural. Ignoring the complex legal and economic system that had grown up, Americans could point to industrial activity as a sphere unto itself, benefiting them, but only so long as it was not "meddled with." If the system were left to run of itself, motor cars and toothpaste would be produced spontaneously in quantity. The onset of depression challenged this view of things, but it took Americans years to grapple with the real complexity of their society. Rather than accept their interdependence they preferred to believe that the economy would "right itself," and they retreated from any analysis of their predicament. In this atmosphere emerged a nostalgic and utterly false image of the 1890's and 1920's as gay and glorious yesterdays free from the tensions and economic difficulties of the 1930's. Similarly, the Model T came to represent youth, springtime, and simple living. It became one with a lost agrarian world.

Americans also created a nostalgic image of Ford that triumphed over reality. Like the car, he also had been a spontaneous product of the economic system, and he stood in opposition to those who would regulate it, whether through unions or government. His popularity was greater than any other leader's in May 1937, when *Fortune* conducted a special survey of labor opinion among both organized and unorganized labor. Asked "Which of these people do you feel have been on the whole helpful to labor and which harmful?" 73.6% chose Ford, while Senator Wagner (51%), Secretary of Labor Perkins (43.4%), the Chairman of General Motors Alfred Sloan (25.5%), President of the United Mine Workers John L. Lewis (32.6%), and Socialist candidate for president Norman Thomas (14.1%) all trailed far behind.[15] The strength of Ford's support is astonishing only if one assumes that public thinking changes rapidly and rationally in response to new conditions. However, the whole Depression era is evidence to the contrary.

More than changed conditions were necessary before Ford's appeal to American workers would be transformed. A real loss of faith in the "natural" economic system was necessary before many would change their view. Faith in the "natural" economic system existed in Roosevelt's own brain trust, while the president himself pursued a vacillating course between managing the economy and allowing it to struggle without planned government interference. Only in April 1938 did Roosevelt endorse wholeheartedly the deficit spending that many advisors had been urging for several years.[16] Unionization followed a similarly uneven course, again reflecting unwillingness to conceive of regulation of the economy as the proper solution, this time at the individual level. Generally, despite a number of successful strikes in 1934, unionization was successful only between 1936 and the outbreak of war in 1939.

In December 1936 the first "Big Strike" began, against General Motors, and lasted until victory in mid-February. Other auto manufacturers, General Electric, U. S. Steel, RCA, and Firestone also surrendered in 1937, leaving the Ford Motor Company as the last giant corporation with an open shop. From 1933 to 1935 Ford had refused to join Roosevelt's National Recovery Administration plan, losing millions of dollars in government contracts rather than submit to federal regulation, and he likewise resented attempts to organize his plant. In May 1937, when the unionization movement had already conquered most of Ford's competition, Walter Reuther, Richard Merriweather, and Richard Frankensteen attempted to hand out leaflets at the Rouge Plant. Accompanied by a number of press photographers they climbed the iron steps to an overpass which workers crossed after their shift.

As they prepared to hand out their leaflets, several Ford Security men, including two wrestlers and an ex-boxer, marched toward them and announced, "This is Ford property. Get the Hell off of here." In Allan Nevins' words, "The union men moved toward one of the exits to obey. But they suddenly saw it blocked by other approaching guards, and as they paused were swiftly slugged from behind."[17] Ford men kicked Reuther in the face and threw him down the steps, broke Merriweather's back, and pummeled a woman in the stomach, while photographers watched in horror.

The "Dearborn Massacre" of 1932 had battered Ford's image, generating three other images, but these had receded somewhat in the nostalgia of sentimental pastoralism during the next four years as the economy gradually recovered. The "Battle of the Overpass," as it came to be called, combined with a long slide into further depression which began in August 1937, shifted attention back to what had been minority opinions held by self-conscious conservatives, liberals, and radicals. From increasingly polarized perspectives Americans watched Ford's factories torn with tension and violence. "The last rugged individualist" was making his stand, in his factories in Dallas, Kansas City, and Dearborn, where union organizers were met with fists and blackjacks. During the next three years, when the unions were unable to mount an effective strike because they were beset with internal conflict, a new term came into the industrial workers' vocabulary—"Ford Terror."

In sharp contrast to Ford's popularity among workers before 1929, resentment and even hatred grew more common. Ten years later, the

*United Auto Worker* printed a Ford worker's doggerel that expressed common sentiments.

> But I wonder if those up in heaven
> Ever look down from above
> And see guns, tear-gas and nightsticks
> A symbol of Ford's brand of love?

> Do you think, Henry Ford, you exploiter,
> You can buy with this kind of stuff
> The thanks and goodwill of thousands
> Who haven't nearly enough?

The *UAW* also sponsored Upton Sinclair's "story of Ford America," *The Flivver King* (1937), distributing over 200,000 copies. One of the most widely read books of the labor movement, Sinclair's account emphasized Ford's individualistic pioneer background in a manner strikingly like the *New Republic*'s analysis in 1932. After a surprisingly sympathetic account of Ford's early struggles, Sinclair emphasized the inevitable corruption caused by his vast fortune and power, and concluded:

A billion dollar industrial empire such as Ford's could be met and matched by only one thing, a union of the two hundred thousand Ford workers, controlled by the democratic will of its membership. That was what they meant to have, because it was the only way out of misery and despair for the producing masses.

This belief was worked out in more detail in *Fordism* (1937), Carl Raushenbush's pamphlet for the League for Industrial Democracy. *Fordism* concentrated on the infamous Service Department and described the Overpass incident by way of illustration. Throughout, Ford himself received less attention than his organization. To a leftist, structure and function appeared more important than leadership; the first part of the study demonstrated the ways in which the company prevented "any measure of industrial democracy," and the second part focused upon how "the Ford company subverts political democracy for company aggrandizement." Raushenbush's work was analytical where Sinclair's was passionate, and it focused on the company rather than on Ford. But both came to the same conclusion: unionization was essential to preserve democracy and "our ancient liberties." Each saw Ford as a victim of the system he had created, caught in historical forces beyond his control.[18]

Inevitably, however, as Hitler rose to power and declared war, attacks on Ford became more personal. American Jews remembered his anti-Semitic *Dearborn Independent* and found that its former editor, William Cameron, had a new vehicle for his prejudice in the "Anglo-Saxon Federation," which still sold the *Protocols of the Elders of Zion.* Cameron remained in Ford's employ, and this fact coupled with the gestapo tactics of the Ford Service Department led many to identify Ford as a native Nazi.

Without actually calling Ford a Nazi, the Friends of Democracy issued a thirty-page newspaper entitled "Henry Ford Must Choose," with those words stretched between the American flag in one corner and a swastika in the other. In his introduction Robert Sherwood praised Ford as "probably the world's greatest genius in industrial mass production." However, "combined with his mechanical genius is an emotional ingenuousness, an intellectual sterility, a rustic narrow-mindedness—a general goofiness—which make him a supreme easy mark for the international gangsters."

The paper alternated between the presentation of facts, such as Hitler's admiration for Henry Ford recorded in *Mein Kampf,* and demands that Ford "take action in the courts to insure that his name no longer be used by the Nazi movement both here and abroad. If he refuses to do so, he stands self-condemned." All in all Ford's earlier pacifism which many believed had hampered American preparedness for World War I, combined with his anti-Semitism to create a picture of at least unintended Nazi collaboration.[19]

Ford's battle with the UAW and CIO culminated on April 1, 1941, in a spontaneous strike that paralyzed his plant. As the reminiscences of autoworkers show, Ford continued to rely upon Bennett and his strong-arm tactics until near the end of the strike. Perhaps worker feeling is best summed up in a short song one of them composed:

> Once in Dearborn City
> Our Boss Henry Ford
> Thought he was appointed
> To represent the Lord

> But we struck and showed him
> On Heigh Hey Heigh Ho
> We are the Lord's annointed
> Represented by the C.I.O.[20]

As these words suggest, Ford had been completely stripped of his messianic garments, which were now worn by the unions. Industrial salvation was still the ultimate goal, but the means to attain it had changed. And those opposing Ford did not merely envision themselves as fighting for better working conditions, but could identify their struggle with beleaguered democracy both at home and abroad.

No local, state or federal enforcement agency would intervene on Ford's behalf, and with all the roads into his Rouge Plant blockaded, he had little choice but to give in to the strike. The reversal of his image from a secular messiah to a kind of devil was nearly complete, as 97% of Ford's workers voted for either the UAW or AF of L, rejecting his leadership. Beaten, Ford acceded to every union demand and added the check-off of dues from paychecks, ensuring the union's strength. After the strike the apocalyptic visions of Ford as an exploitative capitalist or an American Nazi receded. That they had never predominated became quickly apparent.

While some had suspected Ford of Nazi collaboration, until 1939 a majority of Americans opposed involvement in any future European conflict. As late as 1938, the House came within twenty-one votes of passing the Ludlow amendment, which provided that unless the country were invaded, war could be declared only by a majority in a national referendum. Public opinion shifted rapidly after war began, however, and because Ford also prepared for war, his image changed dramatically. The interests of industry and government became nearly identical again, as they had appeared to be in the 1920's.

By March 1942 Ford was on the cover of *Time* magazine with the caption "Mass Producer: Out of enormous rooms, armies will roll and fleets will fly." A nation suddenly at war relied upon the assembly line and the automotive industry. *Time* praised Ford because long before Pearl Harbor he had already begun converting his factories to war production and because he had begun producing aircraft engines before even receiving the orders for them. Ford had also begun constructing the largest room in the world—his Willow Run Plant—before officially learning that he would assemble planes. He produced amphibious jeeps, trucks, and tanks.

Ford became an exemplar of American productivity. To win the war and also to produce for domestic wants after winning it, "the nation will need . . . more men like Henry Ford: individualistic, cocky, lively, curious and productive." Further, *Time* resurrected the old formula to account for the Ford enigma.

Even the most whole-souled mechanic takes some time off, and Henry Ford, the lean Midwesterner with a farmer's flair for opinionating and a mechanic's scorn for words, was always two men. He was a cantankerous, stubborn, cracker-box philosopher who could not bear to be contradicted; and he was a maker, a maker of machines that work.

Ford the cracker-barrel philosopher had opposed World War I. But as soon as the United States got into the war, "Ford the mechanic got to work. . . ." In this way Ford's social ideas were relegated to a minor position; rather than attempt to see Ford as an integrated personality, *Time* simply split him in two. This procedure says as much, of course, about *Time* and its readers as it does about Ford. Significantly, such social consequences of his ideas as the "Dearborn Massacre" were conveniently omitted from the story, while his more recent labor troubles were only briefly alluded to.

Also gone was Ford the senile antiquarian. Freed of nagging images of Ford, the article expatiated on the wonders being performed by United States industry, using Ford as its exemplar. In the "Battle of Detroit" there was to be "a new reenactment of the old American miracle of wheels and machinery, but on a new scale . . . a miracle of war production. . . ." Where Stidger had been forced to strain a bit to find a suitable miracle in Ford's foundry, no such difficulties appeared in wartime. Stidger had declared that men were produced in the factories; now the machines were made human. Anthropomorphism ran through the article. Bombers were "born from half-mile assembly lines" "coughing with life," and "the deadly infants" were stored on a new airfield. "From those runways the new-born bombers will make their test flights. . . ."

Even more revealing, the managers who supervised their construction were themselves described as mechanical, greasy men with blunt fingers, contemptuous of formality. Paramount among them stood Ford. "His body is still tough, his bright eyes dart restlessly as the fingers of a machine."[21] In this metaphoric confusion Ford passed from the public stage, giving way to his grandson, who succeeded him during the war. In the years immediately preceding his death, few concerned themselves with resolving the lingering contradictions of his character.

Then a new figure emerged at death. Some, to be sure, paid scant attention to that event. *Time* allotted him less than a column inch. Those who wrote more extended obituaries, however, created a new after-image of Ford, in keeping with their own concerns. Sigmund Diamond found, in a survey of those notices in *The Reputation of American Businessmen,* that at his death Ford became a symbol of free enterprise and the capitalistic system. At a time of increasing tension with the Soviet Union, this should not be surprising, yet that final symbolic creation bore no more relation to the man himself than the anachronistic pioneer of the early 1930's or the common man writ large of the 1920's. As Diamond concludes:

With respect to Henry Ford, the verdict of the press was as clear as it was decisive. In his life the American people might see dramatic confirmation of two fundamental precepts: the entrepreneur was linked to the community by the common attributes of humanity and by principles of motivation which guided his activities in the direction of service to all . . . the entrepreneur and the social system were inseparable.[22]

At death Ford again stood for the union of free enterprise and social welfare, foreshadowing the temper of the 1950's. His image, fragmented in the 1930's, was reassembled for the Cold War.

Henry Ford was an original. No matter what avatar he assumed, he was never consistently identified with another figure, but stood alone as a new kind of American hero. Unlike Franklin Roosevelt, who self-consciously assimilated himself to the Lincoln image, after finding Jefferson unsuitable,[23] Ford was a new symbolic creation. Like a Benjamin Franklin or an Andrew Jackson, he signaled a transformation in the American identity. The protean Franklin broke with Europe politically and psychologically to become a citizen of the New World; Jackson stood for the rejection of European culture in the belief that America had a special mission in the vast continent to be accomplished through indomitable will. Both men resisted scholarly interpretation precisely because they were symbolic.

Modern man, no less than so-called primitive man, thinks by means of symbols transforming the world into a discourse. The public determined Ford's symbolic meaning. Despite his statements about reincarnation, he was made into an expression of the dominant culture and its concerns. Through Ford, Americans thought out their conception of the relation between business and government, their attitudes toward peace and war, their response to technology, and their own chances for success.

Franklin and Jackson before him had served much the same purpose for their contemporaries, until their public images became so rich with ambiguities that historians found it difficult to grasp the private man. Because social reality is ultimately neither public nor private, but a construction of both, an accurate picture of any important public figure must include both. For if the public used Ford as a symbol of their dreams of success, their shattering Depression and the fiery consummation of war, he also incorporated the American public and these same events in a private view of the world. Before assessing Ford's meaning for American culture, one must know how he saw his world.

# PART 2

# HENRY FORD'S VIEW OF THE WORLD

*Every new mind is a new classification.*
"Self-Reliance"

*Beware when the great God lets loose a thinker on this planet. Then all things are at risk.* "Circles"

Both passages marked by Henry Ford in Emerson

# CHAPTER FOUR

# I BELONG WITH THE BUDDHIST CROWD

## ORIGINS OF KNOWLEDGE

In 1947 Ford declared "I have come to believe, with Thomas Carlyle, that the chief thing about a human being is his religion." Most who have examined Ford have assumed he was a typical rural Protestant. But Ford believed in reincarnation. He believed that man's thoughts came from a universal brain, that "Somewhere there is a master mind sending brain wave messages to us. . . ." He declared, "I never did anything by my own volition. . . . I was pushed by invisible forces within and without me. We inherit a native knowledge from a previous existence." In short, he was no simple Calvinist. Ford first encountered the doctrine in 1901 and became convinced of its soundness by the end of that year. Along with the belief in reincarnation went the following propositions: that the universe was boundless; that time had no beginning or end; that the essential core of life was indestructible; and that through his various incarnations, man made his own heaven or his own hell. Furthermore, he thought reincarnation offered "an intelligent explanation of the inequalities of life, of the differences in wisdom and maturity of people born into the same world."[1]

Since Ford was hardly a systematic philosopher, the following chapters will examine the practical consequences of these beliefs. Ford never spoke of anything analogous to the "forms," as Platonists use the term, nor did he see the physical world as a veil of maya, as Buddhists conceive it. Instead, he saw the perfect always in the future, assembled out of the elements of truth which were already existing but unrecognized. He believed in static elements of truth, which had to be recognized by or communicated to man, thereby leading to progress, or assembly, through time. The more rapid the recognitions, the more rapid the progress. He thought that "we never create anything new, we merely discover something which has already existed." While a Platonist would mean by such a statement that there were permanent spiritual truths which might be discovered through reflection, Ford's idea led to an unceasing activity because everything knowable was present and only awaited use.

Nor did Ford's belief that "we never create anything new" apply only to material objects. He found "no difference between matter and spirit. They are different degrees of fineness in the same thing." Or, as he added on another occasion, "What we call spirit and what we call matter are one, and the All." Perfection did not involve a translation from the physical to the spiritual. Instead, he believed, "the one is becoming the other, through ascent and descent, and both benefit by the process."

The most important channel for this movement was man himself. In Ford's words, "The human mind is a channel through which things-to-be are coming into the realm of things that are."[2] Furthermore, after death, reincarnation preserved the ideas of the previous generation, since the movement from one body to the next took place entirely within one substance. Hence the conclusion that "We inherit a native knowledge from a previous existence."

To an extent, this belief clashed with Ford's declaration that "Every new life is a new thing under the sun"; evidently he believed it was actually quite an old thing under a familiar sun. However, Ford continued, "A young man ought to . . . look for the single spark of individuality that makes him different from other folks, and develop that for all he's worth." Like his favorite author, Ralph Waldo Emerson, Ford believed each man possessed an individual genius. "The single spark of individuality" was bequeathed quite literally from previous incarnations. As one of Ford's intimates put it, "What passes from one generation to another, as he sees it, is the individual human soul."[3]

In his own life Ford attributed his mechanical ability to reincarnated knowledge rather than environment or training. As he noted, "My father was not a mechanic, nor was my grandfather." Yet, "When a boy of sixteen years of age, without mechanical training I was able to take a watch apart and put it together." According to Ford's personal secretary, Ford never claimed any knowledge of who he had been in previous lives, although one unsympathetic biographer reported that Ford believed he had been Leonardo da Vinci. No direct evidence supports this, although Ford's notebooks do contain ample proof of his general beliefs.[4]

Previous lives were but one source of knowledge; other ideas came directly from the "Universal Brain." Ford held two contradictory views of this source. One was deterministic: "I never made a mistake in my life. Neither did you. Neither did anybody else." All actions were guided; even murder resulted because both murderer and victim needed the experience. The only purpose in living was "to get experience. That's all we get out of life." But Ford did not stick to the determinism implied in these remarks, and he also explained the origin of thoughts another way.

How do we think? What makes us think? Where do our thoughts come from? . . . As with a properly tuned antenna, thoughts seem to come to those ready to receive them. That seems to be the way we get ideas, but it takes a conscious effort on our part to be ready to receive them.[5]

In other words, while Ford held to the idea of a universal brain, or a central guiding consciousness, its messages only came "when we put ourselves into the right mental condition to receive them." The analogy with radio transmission was not accidental. Ford believed the self was "the center of numberless millions of entities making up the thing we call 'I'"; and "that we function not only on the planes that we see, but on others we do not see . . ."

Putting it more graphically, Ford went on, "We are central stations with myriads of entities going and coming all the time with messages." These entities clustered around a central part of the self which carried on from one incarnation to the next; this organizing cell Ford likened to a queen bee. In his next life Ford expected "to retain this central cell, or whatever it is, that is now the core of my personality."[6]

The concept of the mind as a well-tuned receiver dominated Ford's thoughts. Nor was it entirely inconsistent with the deterministic belief that no one ever made mistakes, but was guided, even in apparent adversity. The two ideas differ only in assigning more or less influence to the Universal Brain. Ford leaned toward the view that only some people were "in tune with the infinite," especially himself, but when apparently making a mistake he quickly reverted to the notion that all actions were guided. As Dean Marquis observed, Ford's "mind does not move in logical grooves. It does not walk, it leaps."[7] Many times, these hunches, as Ford called them, did not work out, not only in such well-publicized schemes as the Peace Ship, but also in purely industrial decisions. He obstinately believed that direct electric current was preferable to alternating current until he was forced to change all the machinery in his plant to alternating current. The most famous hunch was the Model T, as its phenomenal success became a reenforcing element. To abandon the Model T would involve more than merely changing his mind; giving it up meant the rejection of inspiration.

Ford could rationalize this change only by reverting to the contradiction just noted. The failure of the Model T became an admonitory experience, when he suddenly reverted from being a seer to a plastic instrument of the Universal Brain. Yet Ford's persistence in his belief in intuition suggests that personal experiences confirmed the belief. While it may be easy to discredit Ford by paying strict attention to his logic or pointing to his mistakes, neither procedure disproves the existence of intuitive discovery.

In fact, there are numerous references to Ford's intuitive powers. The *New Republic* commented, "Some lightning flash of the mind, some instantaneous intuition, shows him the path, and he must follow it, sometimes mistakenly, and not listen to the counsel of doubt. . . ." The language here sounds, and perhaps was meant to be, merely metaphorical. But examples of Ford's "instantaneous intuition" did appear. Edmund Wilson reported that with no past experience in such work, "he is said to have been able to appraise at a glance the bridges of the 'Detroit, Ironton, & Toledo' . . ." This in itself, while suggestive, is still not a description of what Ford seemed to be speaking of. However, accounts of Ford's intuitive feats appear more often closer to Detroit. Nevins and Hill report that Ford could tell which of six identical motors would function merely by looking at them. And Edsel once told of sweating for hours over a complex problem with Ernest Kanzler, a fine engineer, when Ford entered the office, asked what was wrong, and gave an answer almost immediately that solved their difficulty.[8]

Ford's intuition and belief in reincarnation were linked, as one explanation for his ability clearly was that he remembered the solution to problems encountered in previous lives. An alternative explanation of such instantaneous problem solving may be found in the works of such an important mathematician as Poincaré, or such poets as Stephen

Spender and Jean Cocteau, who each describe discoveries which might be called inspirations but which arose because they had already saturated their minds with information before an unconscious process presented a solution.[9] One need not accept Ford's belief in reincarnation in order to believe that he had intuitive experiences.

However, the belief in reincarnation may not be dismissed lightly either. William Butler Yeats, Plato, and Emerson all entertained the idea. Reincarnation does allow for an intelligible explanation of the world based upon its initial premise. In one of his last published interviews, Ford repeated his own belief that "Intelligence and Law" in the universe were "behind its smooth running. . . . Intelligence in control of it." It was, of course, a universe without any dichotomy between body and soul, one where the infant hardly appeared with his mind a *tabula rasa,* or blank sheet of paper. It followed that "natural law and spiritual law are one and the same," since they both dealt with the same substance.[10]

This conception of an orderly universe appears to contradict Ford's belief in an active intelligence sending out explicit information. How can one reconcile a set of general laws with direct intervention in individual minds? Such an active intelligence would appear to violate its own laws. In part, of course, Ford spent little time attempting to harmonize the various elements of his philosophy. Yet at least part of the answer to this apparent contradiction is that the only activity of such an intelligence was to reveal its laws to those prepared to receive them. Thus, through inspiration the process of creation, or progress, would be hastened but not changed.

Some such notion may lie behind the Ford museum at Greenfield Village. Ford's museum and his various restoration projects have usually been interpreted as an attempt to atone for his famous remark "History is bunk." But since his belief in reincarnation was fully developed long before he began these projects, another interpretation seems more plausible. Rather than an atonement for a hasty remark, Ford's Greenfield Village represents a special sense of history that deemphasizes politics, warfare, and the liberal arts. Instead, Ford focused on social and technological history, displaying the implements of everyday life, vehicles representing the history of transportation, clocks and other timepieces, and the skills of craft industry. The buildings he chose to preserve were those where the airplane or electric light had been invented, where Stephen Foster allegedly wrote his songs, and the schoolroom used by McGuffey, author of the most popular textbooks of the nineteenth century.

Ford also preserved examples of every mechanical contrivance. Because "Everything has been here in the world always, just waiting for someone to pick it up and use it,"[11] Ford felt that no earlier inventions should be lost.

It should not be surprising that in addition to the knowledge gained from previous lives, the Universal Brain, and inventions, Ford believed in mental telepathy, or the exchange of entities between people. Brain waves moved not only from the central consciousness of the universe, but between men.

## CARE OF THE BODY

As a corollary to these ideas about mental processes, Ford also had unusual notions about the body. Believing that the soul and body were not split did not lead him to etherealize the body, but rather led him to see it as a boiler, which must not be improperly stoked with alcohol or polluted with tobacco, lest the ability to receive messages from the Universal Brain be impaired. Furthermore, the body must work, since "Men wear out when idle, just as machines do." To prevent the rusting of joints and decay of parts was essential, and consequently, health became one of Ford's major concerns.

Overeating and indulgence in the wrong foods were frequent targets of his scorn. He thought "Most men dig their graves with their teeth," and declared "It isn't work that kills men . . . It's eating—just the way you ruin a boiler if you let it choke up with too much coal and cinders and dirt." Ford explained, on another occasion, that ". . . most of the ailments of people come from eating too much, or eating wrong things. I even go so far as to think a great deal of crime is due to this, as well as despondency. Ailments are caused by, if not entirely due to faulty eating."[12] Ford also made an emphatic connection between diet and world affairs:

The fate of the world—the peace of the universe—rests on its breakfast table. The answer . . . is food, the right kind of food. The question of

food is the most vital problem facing the world today. . . . Analyze the
cause of war and disagreements between individuals. And the answer?
You will find it lies in the petty rivalry of dyspeptic statesmen.

Character was formed by diet; illness was a potential sign of criminality;
war was caused by dyspepsia.

Those who ate properly should live one hundred years, however.
Ford followed the "system" of a legendary Venetian nobleman, Cornaro,
who had only regulated his eating after reaching complete dissipation at
age thirty-five. "All the world knows what happened. In a year he was
well. . . . He lived to be more than 100 years old. . . . Cornaro had a poor
constitution, which he abused. I have never been dissipated."[13] Confident
of his health, Ford followed Cornaro's practices of carefully observing
which foods agreed with him and eating nothing else, and of eating
only when he felt hungry, sometimes in the middle of the night.

These experiments led him to the search for better foods. He thought
". . . maybe we won't be eating the same kinds of food in ten years that
we use now. Science may find that our present foods are not right at
all. . . ." In 1922 he told the *New York Times* he had discovered a new
kind of flour which would enable users to live 100 years. Later his
interest shifted to soybeans, and his laboratories did much of the
original American research and development of soy products. Ford was
interested not only in the soybean as a good source of protein easily
grown by the farmer, but as a useful industrial product. In one of his
enigmatic notebooks he wrote, "Foster whole wheat, whole soy."[14]

Throughout his life, diet consumed much of his time. Ford insisted
on raw milk, liked wheat germ, and believed Vitamin E was an important element of nutrition. He also thought that the crystals in sugar were
responsible for many of the ills of the human body, and wanted his re-
searchers to show him this under the microscope. He became an advo-
cate of artificial milk formed from natural grains, eschewed coffee and
tea, and searched for meat substitutes. In 1926 he told the *New York
Times* that no one should drink milk after the age of eight, and by 1930
was asserting that one should have only one type of food at each meal—
fruit for breakfast, protein for lunch, and starch for dinner. At the 1934
Chicago Exposition the Ford Company served a complete meal of soybean products, including soy-meat and soy-milk. This public display
underscored Ford's concern with the diet of other Americans. In a
*Redbook* interview Ford had assailed the nation's churches for failing

to make diet "a part of religion." Since crime and disease were "the result of wrong mixtures in the stomach," it was essential that clergymen attend to their congregation's eating habits and stop gluttony.[15]

As he had once written in his notebooks, "Churches should be schools," and diet was one fundamental to be taught. This followed logically enough from Ford's belief that "the chief thing about a human being is his religion." Any improvement of society would clearly have to center on the churches working in conjunction with industry. Hence the full quotation from Ford's diary reads "Churches should be schools, Non-sectarian shops near to make tools."[16] The spiritual and the physical would be melded together institutionally.

While such a union was never achieved in fact, Ford did attempt to reform the workmen of his plant, beginning with the famous Five Dollar Day and its concurrent sociological department. He strictly enforced no-smoking rules and rigorously followed Prohibition laws. In early days Ford had been somewhat tolerant of occasional drinking, but by 1920 he had become an absolute opponent of alcohol. As one headline put it, "No breath of rum in the Ford works,"[17] and although the pun was probably unintended, both senses of the phrase were true.

While overhauling the workers, Ford also carried out his own program. He exercised daily, bicycling or taking long walks. To work out problems, he disappeared into the large woods surrounding his Dearborn estate. Often he would walk down the railroad tracks alone to work, despite the protests of his security guards. Until long after his sixtieth birthday he skated during the winter on his estate.

Ford, who ate as little as his friend Thomas Edison, was never anything but lean. Perhaps in hopes of developing the talents of his executives, he began to promote his eating habits among them. Through their reminiscences Sidney Olson drew a composite picture of Ford's luncheons.

Those years of his experimental food theories were sheer misery to his hearty, steak-loving associates. In those years, an invitation to lunch with him was almost equivalent to an invitation from an Inquisitor. . . . lunch consisted of what Henry blithely called "roadside greens." These were simply assorted weeds, variously prepared as salads, or lightly boiled, or even stewed—and often appearing in sandwiches. There is nothing quite like a dish of stewed burdock, followed by a sandwich of soybean bread filled with milkweeds, to set a man up for an afternoon's work.[18]

In addition to these gastronomic ordeals, Ford's subordinates often found themselves challenged to high-kicking contests, as Ford agilely snapped his foot above their heads. On other occasions lunch was followed by an old-time dancing session, as Ford kept a fiddler and accompanying musicians on call for this exercise.

Harvey Firestone and John Burroughs found that Ford was never satisfied with merely chopping wood or taking a good walk, and often challenged members of the party to foot races and high-kicking contests as well. Or he might hurry up and down a stream to determine a good mill site. His enthusiasm for making his firewood was expressed in an inscription over his fireplace in the Field Room at Fairlane— "Chop your own wood and it will warm you twice."

Even more important, of course, was Ford's ambition to remain youthful. A jotbook entry said, "neotreist [*sic*] neoterist, one who stays young / one who stays young."[19] Whatever the merits of these diets and exercises singly, Ford lived to be eighty-three. When one recalls that Ford supervised the creation of the Model A when he was sixty-five, and that he was seventy when he battled Roosevelt over NRA plans, his vigor is almost astonishing. And when one realizes that he outlived his son Edsel and many of the executives who spurned the roadside greens at his table, it is hard to dismiss all Ford's dietary habits.

These habits were to maintain energy. When Ford didn't describe the body as a boiler he often said that "man is just a human storage battery, that's all." The longer one lived, the more the battery could be charged, if kept in good condition. "Every bit of experience is an added charge of power . . . ," he said, and one "ought to keep on charging right up to the end of his life. . . ." Thus, as he explained to John Reed, "What are we here on earth for? Only to get experience. A man is born when he wants to, and dies when he wants to; and the only time he's in trouble is when he isn't getting experience." Thus, to the argument that "you can't take it with you" Ford would retort that one could take the experience of life along, in effect saying that man was in control of his destiny, even to the point of deciding his birth and death. With such assumptions, Ford cared little for money. Instead, he seemed to have an unquenchable thirst for experience, believing that "the bigger the charge [of experience] you start with the farther you're likely to go."[20]

Following this line of reasoning, Ford concluded aviators would be reincarnated first, since they were in the forefront of progress,[21] and speculated that chickens who fled from approaching cars must have been run over in a previous life. While humorous, these examples show how literally he accepted reincarnation, the transmission of experience charged up in one life to the next incarnation, and the existence of "a master mind sending brain wave messages to us."

Ford's ideas about the mind and body extended outward to his conception of the universe. The microcosm of man was homologous to the cosmos. The universe was set in a certain direction, and man's purpose was to help it move in that direction. ". . . when you go along with it, that is 'goodness.' If you don't, you are getting an admonitory kind of experience." The more experience a man had, the greater his charge of power and the less chance that he would act contrary to the intended direction of his universe. Thus experience was both power and preparation.[22] The universe was a great machine whose inner laws could be understood only when one was charged with sufficient experience, either from the present or previous lives, which then enabled one to become an operator of the machinery.

Ford believed that most men did not have sufficient experience, and it followed that he should have as complete a control as possible. "Men are pushed ahead," he decided, rather than moving of their own understanding. "This pressure may sometimes be due to the appearance of a new personality with a new idea, or it may be due to a combination of circumstances too big for any one person to cause or control." This statement echoes his interest in Tolstoy in combination with the antithetical theory of the "great man" or "powerful idea." His jotbook recorded, "There is only one thing stronger than armies and that is an idea whose time has come."[23]

In fact, Ford seemed to alternate between these two conceptions as the moment suited him. Sometimes he was the great man shaping history, at others the victim of circumstances. When launching the Peace Ship, he was to change history; when entering the war effort, he was moved by circumstances. The invention of the Model T was the result of an inspiration destined to reshape the world; its abandonment was caused by external circumstances which Ford obstinately tried to ignore. This stubbornness suggests that he leaned toward the "great man" theory, but greatness resided in the ability to be far-sighted, in the correct perception of trends and events. Ford's belief in his own intuition and precognition were thus integral parts of his self-confidence. Given these beliefs, he was able to overcome disappointment. Failure was but an "admonitory experience," and he never remained quiet for long, no matter how disastrous his most recent foray had been. After the ignominy of a Mt. Clemens trial he might skillfully outmaneuver his creditors or bid for Muscle Shoals. Ford was not proud, at least in the conventional sense, and it may be helpful to remember that he described himself at Mt. Clemens as an "ignorant idealist." Even that experience was justified by education.

Yet whatever Ford's experiences outside of industry, within his own company he was ever the absolute master, eventually owning not merely a majority of the stock, but placing all of it within his own family. He was free to do as he wished, sometimes in an all too arbitrary fashion, but always in accordance with numerous ancillary purposes. His ideal was to apply knowledge tirelessly, to work and to serve. Mere inspiration was not enough. Action was essential; the time for thinking had passed. As Ford put it to *Good Housekeeping,*

But would Isaiah be writing more Bibles today? . . . He would probably be down in the shops among the workingmen; working over a set of blueprints; remaking the world rather than writing about it. There is no reason why a prophet should not be an engineer instead of a preacher.[24]

Ford saw himself as just such a prophet, reincarnated as engineer, "remaking the world rather than writing about it."

# CHAPTER FIVE

# TO STOP WAR BY DESTROYING COWS

## ORGANIC CONCEPTION OF INDUSTRY

Because Ford held that laws operated in the universe and that the universe was "set" in a particular direction, one might expect from him a mechanistic and competitive view of business. Nothing was further from Ford's conception. In fact, he repeatedly said that "If competition were introduced into all industrial groups, it would destroy all productive processes. Cooperation and not combative competition is the basis of progress." While such ideas may seem naive for any businessman in the 1920's, recent economic historians such as Gabriel Kolko have advanced the argument that it was precisely such a "combative competition" which drove the robber barons to form trusts.[1] Ford was, then, to some extent describing contemporary reality.

In practice he opposed competition by sharing "trade secrets," allowing other companies to visit his plant and learn of his production methods. Nor was Ford's generosity limited by national boundaries or politics. In an era when fear of Bolshevism was rampant and Eugene Debs was in prison, Ford freely gave aid to the Russians. When the Communists asked for help in tractor production, he sent parts, blueprints, and trained executives to aid in the establishment of Russian factories.

Ford's internationalism was no accident or whim. It had been expressed earlier in the Peace Ship, and he was a professed internationalist who hoped that national borders would be obliterated by economic considerations. He felt that the ability to travel in inexpensive motor cars would help put an end to national differences. As isolation broke down when men intermingled, the desire to fight would also be destroyed. Although armies could also use such motorized transport, this aspect of the matter did not seem to bother Ford. In essence his ideas were much like those of Marshall McLuhan. Ford saw the emergence of "a new era" ushered in by "books, mechanics, commerce, and science, the motor car, the radio—all have helped us on the way." Like McLuhan he foresaw a "new thinking and new doing . . . bringing us a new world, a new heaven, and a new earth. . . ."

Barriers between race and nationality were also attacked in Ford's language school, where 2,200 foreign-born employees studied English. Its graduation exercises graphically revealed the school's purpose, "Across the back of the stage was shown the hull and deck of an ocean steamship docked at Ellis Island." In dim light "a picturesque figure appeared at the top of the gangway. Dressed in a foreign costume and carrying his cherished possessions wrapped in a bundle suspended from a cane," each graduate in turn descended into "an immense caldron across which was painted the sign 'Ford English School Melting Pot'" holding a sign indicating the country he had come from. Minutes later, the figures emerged in turn from the Melting Pot "dressed in American clothes, faces eager with the stimulus of new opportunities. . . . Every man carried a small American flag in his hand."[2]

As the example makes clear, Ford's internationalism should not be confused with toleration for cultural variation. For him the metaphor of the melting pot included not only the homogenization of foreigners in America, but the mechanization and standardization of people all over the globe. Men would be mass produced. The "new heaven" and "new earth" would be White Anglo-Saxon Protestant. It would be entirely concrete, requiring but the translation of experience into new machines. Nor was Ford's brand of internationalism mere rhetoric, as the Russian example suggests. During American differences with Mexico in 1917 he suggested solving their problems with a factory, "to give them something to do." Factories were established in England, France, Brazil, and Germany, with smaller assembly units in other countries.

Ford also expressed his internationalism by the Peace Ship, of course, and during the 1930's became interested in the Moral Rearmament Movement. He stopped short of becoming a member, however, and when the group failed to pay its bill after a conference at his Dearborn Inn, Ford decided he could not afford Moral Rearmament.

For the most part he concentrated on American business. Here his organic conception of industry was worked out. His methods and machines were sent abroad; but the focus was always in Detroit. A good example of his attitude toward industry is the manner in which he acquired the Johansson gauges and blocks. Developed by an immigrant from Sweden, Carl E. Johansson, they were the most accurrate measuring devices then available. Ford bought Johansson's company, moved it to Detroit, and began using the gauges in all aspects of car production. He refused to keep them to himself, however, arguing that that would be short-sighted. Ford declared that "The better the workmanship of the country in general, the better will be our automobile and tractor sales."

For if all products were made with the finest precision possible, they would last longer, freeing more money to be spent on new goods instead of merely replacing those which were defective and quickly worn out. The additional money which was no longer caught in the cycle of replacement would enable men to buy goods they had never owned before, such as motor cars. Thus, he concluded, "Every waste cut out somewhere in business helps the whole body of business."[3]

In other words, Ford wanted the very antithesis of planned obsolescence in his product. It seemed impossible to build anything too well; the better it was, the longer it lasted, and the more money was free to purchase new goods. Ford believed that any waste in a business system slowed it down; most wasteful of all were those who did no work, the "parasites" who lived on the work of others because the money system was organized in their favor.

Ford attacked the parasites through anti-Semitic articles in his *Dearborn Independent;* he attacked waste and inefficiency with his famous Five Dollar Day. Many different theories have been advanced to explain the sudden introduction of the high wage policy, most of which originated with Ford himself. In *My Life and Work,* coauthored with Samuel Crowther, he described it as an act of social justice. But E. G. Pipp, for a time editor of the *Dearborn Independent,* declared that with a speed-up Ford saw he could make more despite the high wage. Yet another interpretation was advanced by Dean Marquis, who recalled that Ford wished to pay the minimum salary necessary for good family living.[4] However, a fourth interpretation embracing the other three seems possible. Given Ford's abhorrence of waste and desire to quicken the implementation of his ideas, the introduction of higher wages was a method to achieve both ends. Ford argued that well-paid employees would be careful of their tools, report possible problems or improvements, work harder, and so forth. Further, "the whole body of business" would be aided by higher wages in any one sector. Workers would be able to buy the cars they made. By regarding the Five Dollar Day as an act directed against waste and designed to speed up progress, the previous three interpretations all fit together. The speed-up, in this perspective, becomes an act of social justice designed to improve wages and family life.

Yet perhaps the most striking example of Ford's encouragement of national industry, although less well known or applauded than the high wage policy, was his refusal to endorse the patent system. Not only did he give competitors free access to this plant, allow anyone to use the Johansson blocks and gauges, and initiate the Five Dollar Day and the five-day week, Ford also agreed with Edison that patents should not be taken out at all, because secrecy and exclusiveness in industry would slow progress and breed distrust. Since Ford believed that nothing was really new anyway, why allow anyone to claim the right to a particular machine or process?

These attitudes were reenforced by the famous Selden Patent Case which Ford had fought throughout the early years of his corporation's existence. After Ford had been threatened by the Association of Licensed Automobile Manufacturers, it is not hard to see why he opposed monopolies based upon patent claims. Patents helped form monopolies rather than protect inventors, and they inhibited experience and the capacity for service. For service was as important to Ford as his attacks on all forms of waste. He always contended that those who worked solely to make money rather than give service would find business difficult, while if the main purpose were to serve the public, money would take care of itself. This ideal was more than mere rhetoric, as the constantly declining cost of the Model T attested. He often spoke of service and new markets together, but when the new markets disappeared in 1929, so did much of the Ford service, if measured in terms of higher wages and lower car prices.

The ideal of service, like the high value he placed on progress, implicitly assumed an unlimited expansion into a new world which consisted of raw materials. Any check on expansion, whether in the form of patents, waste, improper diet (wasting food and men), alcohol, international bankers, or other "parasites" had to be opposed. Education had to be turned toward production; Ford jotted in his notebook, "Everyone work on mass production/ can be taught very quickly." The assembly lines must move faster. More cars must be sold for less while workers were paid more each year. As one of Ford's longest notebook entries reads,

a car for the masses
one in every home family
no licqur, big army and navy
nothing will do as much to make good roads
as a car in every family good (cars?
will get people to the country
farm produce can be transported and
reduce the cost of (?)
and enable feeling to trans
mixes people and educate them
in small facilities
    The way to make many men do a little work is to
do more yourself, think and help your employees the
more you help the more he will have to do and the
sooner he will becomb one of you
*[spelling, punctuation, and length of lines unchanged]*

Thus mass production, deurbanization, prohibition, and the service ideal were interrelated in Ford's mind. As he once said to the *New York Times,* "if the prohibition laws were changed we'd have to shut up our plants. Everything in the United States is keyed to a new pace. . . ."[5] Incredible as this statement may seem, it is comprehensible within the framework of the service ideal with its emphasis on eliminating waste and hurrying mass production.

### THE FORD PLANT

    Within his own plants Ford checked any tendencies toward waste in materials or inefficiency among men. He prohibited smoking, and drinking was severely punished, often with immediate dismissal. Workers whose homes met the standards of his Sociological Department were eligible for special benefits. If a family rented rooms to boarders, they were not eligible for the highest pay scales. The habit of saving was encouraged by giving high interest rates through a payroll savings plan. Ford was sure that most people would prefer to live his way if only they experienced it. For a time he tried to force all workers to farm some land in addition to doing their regular jobs. They would thus save money, exercise in the outdoors, and keep in touch with the soil. These activities would promote efficiency in the human machines and accelerate production.

Eliminating material waste was no less important, and Ford's scheme for "burning coal twice"[6] was only one example. The first burning created coke while all gases and other by-products released by this process were utilized in the production of cars. Coal dust and sawdust were swept from the floors and burned as well, while all metal scraps were recycled in the Ford blast furnaces. Even the boxes used for shipping motors were reused, to make wooden panels on Ford cars.

The culmination of this desire to control and use everything efficiently was the River Rouge Plant—the largest automobile plant ever constructed, covering several square miles of somewhat marshy land outside Detroit. Here Ford concentrated every process and made every part necessary to manufacture his Model T. Here no space or time were wasted. By 1923 it took but forty-one hours from the moment iron ore left a barge on the Rouge River slip until a Model T was driven off at the other end of the assembly line under its own power.[7] Efforts were constantly made to speed production. Work was further subdivided and the assembly line moved faster each year, as Ford drove the workers, believing himself to be driven by "unseen forces within and without."

While one sympathetic observer called work on the line a "kind of modern dance," few workers echoed him. Labor turnover rose in the 1920's despite good wages. Men did not leave solely because of the speed-ups. Tension mounted in the plant as Model T sales dropped, key executives left, and Ford became more irascible. Just as Ford believed that "Purchasers really have to be trained and led as though they were an army,"[8] he believed in rigid discipline for his workers. Unable to question his own leadership, since it was "guided," Ford fired those who criticized as business difficulties increased. Instead of changing the Model T, in order to compete with Chevrolet, by adding what he considered to be useless luxuries, Ford attempted to educate the public.

He attacked the new credit buying system as unsound and predicted it would soon die out. He had no sympathy for what Veblen would call conspicuous consumption, and refused to believe that customers could long be led astray by yearly style changes and other gimmicks.

When sales dropped below the two million mark for the first time in three years in 1926, Ford refused to attribute this decline to any failing in his product, but accused the sales department and his dealers of laziness and a poor mental attitude. He became more ruthless in his operation of the plant, and men took over much of the management "whose theory was that men were more profitable to an industry when driven than led, that fear is a greater incentive to work than loyalty."

Thus while Ford's ideals were efficiency, elimination of waste, service before profits, and perfection of mass production, in reality a new breed rose to the top of the Ford plant. Those who stood by him in the crisis were either weak men, unwilling to oppose him, or sycophants who reacted fluidly in response to his commands. Men like Charles E. Sorensen, an iron-willed Dane who followed orders unquestioningly and ruled his subordinates through force came to rule, while executives such as Ernest Kanzler, who preferred a more cooperative management which decentralized responsibility, were forced out of the company, many joining Ford's competitors.

The nature of Ford's plant organization also contributed to the rise of the "scavengers," as Marquis so presciently called them.[9] Perhaps as a result of his early experience in small factories, Ford gave almost no titles to his executives. They were each responsible for as much as they could do within vaguely defined areas. Lines of authority were never established, beyond the obvious fact that Ford's decisions were final. Men like Sorensen could, and did, carve out their own empires, invading the areas controlled by others. Ford reasoned that men should grow into their proper positions in the organization without being hindered by any guidelines. In practice, this meant that executives competed for power, that new managers might be driven by their superiors to see how much they could do, and that middle-level engineers often received contradictory orders. The fluid work boundaries encouraged both personality conflicts and efforts to use Ford's whims and sudden decisions as levers to dislodge rivals or "enemies" within the plant.

Ford felt such competition among insecure executives would exact their utmost energy in implementing new ideas. This notion would seem to contradict his idea that competition in industry at large was undesirable. Outside the factory, competition could lead only to secrecy, shoddy production, and possible monopolies. But inside the plant, competition would ensure that no secrets were kept from Ford, and spur men to complete projects more quickly, especially when they knew that he sometimes commissioned the same job in two different parts of the plant. Thus these contradictory policies outside and within his factory were justified by Ford's ideals of speeding production and eliminating waste.

Ford himself actively supervised the vast Rouge Plant, often spending ten hours a day there. He was seldom in his office, but preferred to wander through the plant, stopping to advise subordinates or discuss a new project with his engineers. In his own words he was "down in the shops among the workingmen; working over a set of blueprints; remaking the world. . . ."

### THE LARGER DESIGN

After the perfection of the Model T, Ford turned to other concerns, confident that the constant improvement of his methods must encompass the life outside his plant. He wished to transform the family life of his workers, their diet, their city life, and their morals, as well as provide them with cheap transportation. Throughout the latter part of his career, Ford stuck to a central idea which these others revolved around, that of moving men back to the countryside to live in a way which combined industrial and agricultural labor. The concrete expression of this idea could be found not only in the Model T, but in the creation of village industries, or small factories along Michigan streams, employing men when their modernized farms did not need attention. Establishing such factories, Ford declared, "will bring about a most remarkable change in the country. We are out of balance and it is necessary that we should get back into balance."

As Ford said to John Reed,

I think the normal life for a man is to get back to the land. The land is the healthiest place to be. The trouble up to now is that a man couldn't get enough experience on the farm; but now, with the telephone, the phonograph, the moving pictures, the automobile . . . the farmer can live in the country and have all the experience in the world.[10]

Americans might now remain in "the healthiest place to be" without being penalized by the loss of experience. This new integration was nothing less than a revival of the Emersonian dream of the whole man. Instead of a society of fragmented functionaries, Ford envisioned each man doing all things. Emerson had articulated this doctrine in "The American Scholar." He wrote,

Man is not a farmer, or a professor, or an engineer, but he is all. Man is priest, and scholar, and statesman, and soldier. In the divided or social state these functions are parcelled out to individuals, each of whom aims to do his stint of the joint work. . . . But, unfortunately, this original unit, this fountain of power, has been so distributed to multitudes, has been so minutely subdivided and peddled out, that it is spilled into drops. . . .[11]

Ford wanted to reconstitute the whole man in a new environment. The village factory would enable men once more to embrace many functions. In time the farmer and worker would disappear to be replaced by a single type who embodied the virtues of both. With machines, farm work could be done in less than one month's time out of the year. Men could then do other things, including factory work, although even the factory might eventually disappear, to be replaced by the use of power tools in the home, where each might carry on the production of a single item. He envisioned an evolution from cottage industry to factory and back to the home, with each shift in location a result of changes in technology.

This larger framework clarifies an apparent contradiction between Ford's practice and his philosophy. For clearly it can be objected that far from getting men back to the country or giving them a new multiplicity of function, Ford in fact brought them to Detroit and mired them in jobs of such dullness and repetition that they became automatons. This contradiction reflects Ford's inability to carry through the process he envisioned. It was arrested at the large factory stage. He did set up some village industries, small factories run by the water power of the streams in central Michigan. But society did not follow him back to the country or clamor for more of these village industries. Instead, perversely, the public demanded a new product—a "better" car. Rather than consciously change the American environment, Ford was forced to invent the Model A and its successors instead of realizing his vision of reintegrating farmer and worker.

His philosophy was counter to the conspicuous consumption, the attraction of big city life, the centralization of culture, and the postwar disillusionment of his times, yet his cars carried men to the city rather than away from it, and his factories made society more interdependent and specialized rather than fostering the whole man. Although Ford's plan failed, it had been worked out in some detail. He did not envision a return to the nineteenth-century vision of Jeffersonian yeoman farmers and the simple life of the soil, but rather sought a complete transformation of social and productive relationships through technology. A graphic example of this intent, reminiscent of Bellamy's *Looking Backward,* was his idea that cooking meals at home was wasteful and would eventually be replaced by larger facilities outside the family. Food would be delivered, hot and ready to eat, more cheaply than it could be made at home—and wives would be freed of this drudgery.[12]

As this example suggests, Ford's ideas, when implemented, have transformed many of the forms of American life. He believed that if mass production, specialization, the service ideal, and the production of permanent goods were all pressed far enough they would harmonize relations among men and between man and nature. The key was proper management. As he said on the company's twenty-fifth anniversary, ". . . principally we have learned to manage. . . . We do not know very much about anything as yet. We still waste more than we use. We waste men, we waste materials, we waste everything. . . ."

Proper management eliminated waste. On the farm these ideas took specific forms. "The horse," he declared, "is one of the crudest machines in the world." And making the same point in another interview, he called horses 1,200-pound hay motors of one horsepower. Not content with replacing the horse by the Model T and Fordson Tractor, by 1921 Ford intended the same fate for the cow.

It is a simple matter to take the same cereals that the cows eat and make them into a milk that is superior to the natural article and much cleaner. The cow is the crudest machine in the world. Our laboratories have already demonstrated that cow's milk can be done away with and the concentration of the elements of milk can be manufactured into scientific food by machines far cleaner than cows.[13]

For if cows, like horses and men, were but machines, it followed that men should make better machines. These new machines would have profound effects. As Ford's notebook recorded his plan, "To stop war by disstroying [sic] cows."

Although Ford wavered on the cow question for a few years—in 1923 he suggested that perhaps more efficient ones might be created—he had nothing good to say of them by the 1930's. He even dismissed their value as steak. "Meat is not essential. . . . A scientific food . . . will not only take the place of milk, but meat." The thinking behind such statements is familiar enough in today's ecological crisis. Ford believed that one could get "a more plentiful supply of food, cheaper and better, by processing the products of the soil instead of asking cows and chickens to do it for us." These were Ford's thoughts in 1936, however, when farms were overproducing, and few Americans could understand any thinking which led to the conclusion that "In the future farm animals of all kinds will be out. We won't need them. We will be better off without them."[14]

Ford strove to make better machines to replace the present ones, whether they were horses, cows, or chickens. Anything wasteful had to be improved. He wished to replace sheep, for example, by using soybean fibre for the production of cloth. He reasoned that "Each year it takes two acres to support one sheep which may produce ten pounds of wool. But these two acres will yield 400 pounds of soybean fibres." Ford himself wore a hat and suit of this "wool" at an interview in 1943, and served his correspondent with soybean milk at lunch.

The elimination of inefficient farm animals suggests the other changes Ford wanted. Just as cloth and milk would come from soybeans, once they were transformed by industrial processes, "every single farm product can be turned to industrial uses . . . it is not only possible, but probable that the new interrelation of agriculture and industry will cause industry to move out into the fields, to be closer to the raw materials."[15] The movement away from the city would be motivated not only by Emersonian ideals, but by economic necessity.

The farms themselves would be transformed as the factories moved out from urban centers. Individual farmers would band together in the larger corporations which complete mechanization required. Fences and their waste of land would be eliminated, along with the farm animals they restrained. The model for these corporate farms could be found near Ford's automobile plant, where he maintained an experimental farm that could be "cultivated and cropped in fifteen days, by men who earn $6 per day."

With the enormous time set free by this corporate arrangement,.men would then turn to the village factory, where their agricultural products could be transformed into industrial goods. As early as 1921, Ford was experimenting with natural materials for car parts, as he told the *New York Times,* which reported the development of a "cottonoid car."[16] Ford's engineers had found a mixture of cotton, glue, and formaldehyde which could be blocked out into car bodies before the tough material hardened. The day of the heavy automobile was apparently over. Ford had always stressed light-weight cars; his Model T was one of the lightest cars on the market, yet even in 1915 he was considering the use of plastics in its construction. He constantly inveighed against the belief that there was any relation between weight and strength. The cottonoid experiments were not isolated efforts; he also experimented with aluminum.

However, his chief interest seems to have been growing materials for car production. The soybean not only provided substitutes for milk, meat, and wool, it also had industrial uses. By 1933 Ford used soy oil for foundry cores, molding compounds (roughly like plastic), and as a synthetic resin in paint finish for his cars.

Applying this experience, Ford declared, "We do not yet know how large a share of a modern automobile can be grown annually on the farm instead of exhausting the mines and forests." Discovering a substitute for metal even in one part of an automobile would save a great deal when multiplied by the number of cars produced annually. "Ford chemist Russell Hudson McCarroll estimated that the use of plastics for interior window moldings alone would increase the company's use of farm-grown metal-substitutes twenty-five million pounds annually. This would decrease the annual requirement of sheet steel much more than the same amount" since it was much heavier. Even more important, farmers would have a market, and the double savings of such projects attracted Ford to the chemurgy movement, "an organized attempt to create true wealth—that only real wealth which lies dormant and neglected in the powers of the soil and the air and the sun and the mighty minds of people."

Ford was an active exponent of chemurgy and was the host at the third convention of chemurgists at the Dearborn Inn in 1937, where he had ample opportunities to demonstrate the various uses of soybeans. He had also experimented with a felted material "on the general order of paper . . . pressed, coated, and formed so that it fits exactly in place,"[17] made from grain straws, corn stalks, and sugarcane pulp. Waste would become part of his cars, transforming chaff into elements of a dynamic process rather than allowing it to molder and sink back into the earth. Management would make all things useful.

Such management would save natural resources. Rather than burn oil, for example, Ford proposed that cars use wood or grain alcohols. One of Ford's associates recalled that this interest had begun during the Highland Park days. Later, in 1919, Ford investigated the plan of a man named Kocher to make alcohol from wood chips. At other times he considered a "straw fuel" experiment and many others. He knew that Germany had successfully used alcohol as a gasoline substitute during World War I, and foresaw potential oil shortages if industrial expansion continued. Similarly, he wished to conserve forests and mines by substituting for woods and metals annually harvested materials which could be converted into plastics and felted or cardboardlike substances. Not only would limited natural resources be saved, but even more important, farm income would be integrated with industrial production.

Industrial concerns which moved to the countryside and joined with farming corporations would provide a balanced economy and a variety of occupations to every man. Cities would disappear; they were doomed. And with them,

"I think farmers are going to disappear in the course of time . . . ," he continued, his face lighting up with a look that was half the look of a seer and half the look of a child. "Yes, and factory workers too. Every man will be a farmer some day, and every man will work in a factory or office. We've proven that already. I've built little factories all along the little rivers. . . ."[18]

## A DYNAMIC STANDARD OF VALUE

After watching Ford on their camping trips together, John Burroughs noted, "With him everything gets back to power." He had seen Ford racing up and down streams in remote areas of Appalachia and New England and knew that Ford "never tired of talking of how much power is going to waste everywhere." With them on these trips were Harvey

Firestone and Thomas Edison. Ford had an extravagant admiration for the inventor, a reverence later expressed in his painstaking reconstruction of the laboratory where the electric light had been invented. He even brought New Jersey red clay from the original site, packing it around the sides of the building.

To Ford, electricity was an endless fascination. He did not claim to understand it, modesty remarkable in a man who had quick answers for most questions. Electricity was the universal expression of power, moving according to regular but mysterious laws at the speed of light, and it could be obtained from earth, air, fire, and water. Ford looked for ways to harness each of these to his purposes.

Ford found the world almost entirely "in the raw material stage," waiting for proper development. This meant careful management of the available resources, not rapid exploitation of them. In fact, Ford seems to have had an ecological sensibility, not only in his emphasis on eliminating waste and in his search for agricultural substitutes for wood and iron, but also in his search for other sources of power which were imperishable. For example, when Ford bought 160,000 acres of coal fields after the rejection of his Muscle Shoals bid, he was determined not to waste any coal. He hoped to burn it underground, saving time and energy otherwise used in hauling it to the surface. That failing, he would burn the coal at the minehead and ship electricity over the wires. To Ford's mind, however, perishable earth materials were the least efficient and most wasteful sources of energy. He would have preferred to harness the winds, which blew uselessly across the states, and so he conducted experiments with windmills. Near his experimental farm he had "a small house at Dearborn which [was] entirely lighted by electricity generated by a windmill."[19] Today this idea is again being implemented in response to the intensifying energy crisis. Ford also expected that men would eventually trap the sun's energy directly rather than rely upon the solar energy preserved in oil and coal or reflected indirectly in the hydraulic cycle.

While the use of air and the sun remained in the experimental stage, however, waterpower was Ford's chief interest. Even before Burroughs had noticed it, and before the famous bid for Muscle Shoals, Ford had purchased interests in other waterpower projects, notably in St. Paul, Minnesota, where he built an assembly plant. He also had a waterpower project in mind for Green Island in the Hudson River. Ford was sure that "There is enough water power on this continent to run railroads, factories, homes—everything; and cheap." In the words of Allan Benson, "A river that is rolling its way to the sea without working is to Mr. Ford a river in disorder."[20]

The Tennessee had been one of the most disorderly of all rivers, flooding many areas as it twisted its way to the Mississippi. Ford planned to tame its waters and use the energy they contained to run factories which would provide fertilizers to impoverished Southern and Midwestern farmers, and then buy back their crops for use in other plants. This project symbolized much more to Ford than industrial expansion or merely a public service to the nation's farmers.

"From the operation of this plant," he said, "many great things are possible, greater power production, the production of aluminum and nitrates in quantities. . . . But all these things are incidental. The one big thing which I see in Muscle Shoals is an opportunity to eliminate war from the world."

Now by what leap of logic, or faith, did Ford see in the Shoals the deliverance of mankind from war? Partly because the nitrates produced could be used to make explosives as well as fertilizer, and that might act as a deterrent. But the principal explanation of how a dam would deliver mankind from war involves Ford's conceptions of power, money, politics, and experience. He regarded his age not as that of machinery, but as the age of power. As he said in 1928, "There are many things more valuable than money—time, energy, and materials. . . ."[21] Proper use of power at Muscle Shoals would conserve all three of these and simultaneously create a new monetary standard of value, which was the key to Ford's whole proposal.

For Ford had uncovered what he regarded as the central cause of war. "The cause of all wars is gold. We shall demonstrate to the world through Muscle Shoals, first the practicability, second the desirability of displacing gold as the basis of currency and substituting in its place the world's imperishable natural wealth." Gold was limited in extent and under the control of a small cartel of international bankers. Gold was static and could only produce wealth because it had arbitrarily been chosen as the international standard of exchange. Gold could only work for its possessors when used as security for large loans with heavy interest payments. Wars were ideal situations for men with gold, for warfare made heavy demands on all capital. Thus wars had to be stirred up and prolonged in order to ensure continuing wealth to the gold mongers. So ran Ford's logic.

He planned to substitute a dynamic imperishable for a static one—to base money on power. "Under the new currency system a certain amount of energy exerted for one hour would be equal to one dollar." An ongoing dynamic process would become the basis for exchange. The government would not borrow money at high interest from bankers, but would issue new money on the basis of the energy potential of Muscle Shoals. To Ford it seemed ridiculous that the same government which issued and ensured the value of currency should also pay for the use of that money in the construction of a project which could itself repay the loan through production. In his words, "Which is more imperishable, the more secure, this power site and its development, or the several barrels of gold necessary to make $40,000,000?"

Given control of this imperishable monetary power, Ford proposed "to complete it, develop it, get it working, and then fix it so it can never be exploited for private ends, but shall always remain in the service of all the people. . . ." With control of money outside the banks and lodged in natural process, control would pass to the people. The "energy dollar" would prevent war by destroying the static power which the international bankers possessed and substituting a dynamic source of wealth. Thus, "In a sense the destiny of the American people for centuries to come lies there on the Tennessee River, because whoever controls a nation's power controls that nation's people."

Once Muscle Shoals proved its practicability, Ford expected universal adoption of his plan, and the damming of every American river and stream, including the entire Mississippi valley. His imagery suggested millennialism: "We could make a new Eden of our Mississippi valley, turning it into the great garden and powerhouse of the country."[22] The garden and the powerhouse would become one.

The American public correctly understood at least this much of Ford's vision. They may never have heard of reincarnation, precognition, the service ideal, or other basic premises of Ford's philosophy, but many did grasp the vision of Muscle Shoals. Where Henry Adams had recognized the existence of two centers of force, one symbolized by the Virgin, the other by the dynamo, Ford now conceived of nature itself as a dynamo waiting to be tamed by man. Horses, cows, and sheep were inefficient machines. Man was a machine. And the world consisted of untapped energies waiting to be harnessed, harmonized, and transformed into a different degree of fineness in the one substance which constituted both matter and spirit. Adams had felt momentarily that he should worship the dynamo; Ford never doubted that faith, and the mass of American people demonstrated their own allegiance to his Model T even after the Muscle Shoals bid failed.

Years earlier Ford's powerhouse in the Highland Park factory had been housed in a spotless building. Through its numerous windows the tiled interior and polished machinery were visible, symbols of Ford's enthusiasm for machinery, cleanliness, and power. Now Ford wished to make a much larger project a similar showpiece. It would put an end to war and its waste; change the standard of monetary value; begin the reunion of farm and factory. Inefficient natural machines would be replaced, and men would no longer be subservient to the city or deprived of experience because they lived on the land. The world would be transformed. Efficiency and elimination of waste would dictate new social relations among the people, relations ensured by a dynamic standard of value.

### ECONOMICS AND POLITICS

Political boundaries and political opinions don't really make much difference. It is the economic condition which really forces change and compels progress.                                        *Henry Ford*

Ford's stress on economics rather than politics sounds reminiscent of Karl Marx, especially when combined with his "energy dollar"—or energy theory of value. Yet the comparison is in fact no more valid than that between Marx and the Jacksonians. Ford himself was a great admirer of Andrew Jackson, and almost symbolically, he visited the Hermitage on his journey to Muscle Shoals. As he said to the *New York Times,* "I would not have missed this for anything. I have promised myself for ten years that I would visit the home of Old Hickory." Ford's admiration was bolstered by readings, as he had purchased "everything that I could get hold of on the life of Andrew Jackson."[23]

With his reading in Emerson and about Jackson, Ford clearly had established ties with earlier American philosophy and politics. He did not, however, parrot earlier theories, no more adopting Jacksonian

banking policy than he had Emersonian ideas about the relation between man and nature. He did not wish merely to demolish a national
bank, as Jackson had done, but to change the fundamental basis of
exchange, which apparently would bring him close to the Marxist
viewpoint.

But despite their agreement on the necessity for a new money system, Ford and Marx disagreed on the role of the state. Where Marx
predicted inevitable socialization of capital and its management by the
state, Ford conceived of an enlightened industrial leadership outside
of politics, a leadership which spread the benefits of production. That is,
quality distribution would be placed before personal profits.

Ford maintained that his monetary surplus represented the public's
investment; consequently he believed he had no right to keep these
monies, but should cut the price of his product, expand productive
facilities, and raise wages rather than take large profits. Where Marx saw
the wage system as inherently vicious and a mechanism for the creation
of surplus value, Ford argued that high wages were profitable, creating
what he called the "wage motive" to achieve higher production with
less waste. Marx predicted that capitalism would periodically over-
produce, flooding markets and throwing men out of work. In contrast,
Ford feared that waste and mismanagement, combined with the gold
standard, would encourage profiteering and the proliferation of shoddy
goods. Such practices were in fact a kind of underproduction, since such
goods were impermanent and needed constant replacement, finally re-
sulting in a loss of public confidence. Further, the very nature of gold
as a static standard of value could easily lead to money shortages if
hoarded. Energy, by contrast, was a dynamic value. As long as the wind
blew, the sun shone, and the waters ran, value would be created.

Thus, despite the apparent similarities between Ford's "energy
dollar" and the labor theory of value, the two theories could hardly be
farther apart. Near the end of Ford's life he expressed the belief that
"We are on the verge of a revolution. Not a proletarian or political
revolution, following the Russian pattern . . . Our revolution will make
political revolution unneeded and impossible." Poverty would be abolished, and "economic maladjustments" would disappear. Rather than
move through political channels, "the changes . . . will touch each citizen, will alter our civilization, because it will revolutionize industry and
agriculture and bring the farmer and city worker in closer contact."

Here is an old Jacksonian belief: that politics are inessential, that once proper economic relations and laws are established, the regulation and expansion of the economy can be safely left in private hands. And just as Jackson had left the presidency stronger and politics more important than ever after eight years in the White House, so Ford was to speed the process of centralization and specialization even as he tried to counteract these tendencies. But unlike Jackson, of course, Ford only toyed with his presidential candidacy, and finally was convinced that he already had the biggest job in the world. He was sincere when he said, in rejecting a candidacy, that he "could do more where I am."[24]

However, before he could attain his goals, Ford had to deal with the banking interests. While there was no class struggle necessary for his economic revolution, there was a struggle; there were enemies. The world was divided between "the real world" and "the world of partisan politics and so-called finance." "The real world of folks, of human values, of material wealth—it is all right." But the bankers and other parasites of the system were another matter. One must stress that Ford's hatred of the banking interests was not personal, as a diary entry reiterated: "not attacing [sic] anyone but the systim [sic]. I don't blame any person but the systim men have been brought up to. . . . I am not fighting any person but the systim." Another note, penciled in the Depression, illustrates his attitudes and their origins.

All wars labor unions strikes by an insiduous [sic] conspiracy. group of war mongers and mongrels for control and greed. i have know of ever sinse [sic] the Selden Patent case 37 years ago
        Clemensau [sic] Wilson
        Lincoln and Booth money system
        Hamilton and Burr

It is clear that Ford entertained a conspiracy theory of history, although the references to various historical figures are unclear. In practice Ford consistently accused unnamed enemies. In 1926, during the British General Strike, he declared that it "was 'put over,' but British labor does not know it. It was jockeyed by the people who are always putting things over, the same people who put over the wars."[25] Capital punishment was also a plan of the financiers. "They want to harden the sensibilities of the people, for it serves their ends to have war." Likewise, unemployment was laid at "the door of the financiers who are chargeable for the thousands of idle men. . . ."[26]

Ford did not consider himself a capitalist or a financier, since he reinvested his profits in the company and kept millions of dollars in the company vaults rather than deposit them in banks. He was a producer, not a parasite. He rejected socialism because it would put non-producers in control, and rejected what he regarded as capitalism for the same reason. Since he was a producer, a man who worked with his hands and employed thousands of others to do the same, social ills could not be attributable to him.

By such logic he could accuse others of fostering unemployment while closing down his own factories for nearly a year and refusing to contribute substantially to relief efforts in Detroit. Ford was against charity because it encouraged men to become parasites in a world of raw materials where much remained to be done. While to others it was evident that closing down the Rouge Plant for a year caused unemployment, Ford did not live in a simple world of cause and effect, but in a moral universe. Shiftless and lazy men might be unemployed, but not men with any vision or energy. Alternately, if good men were out of work, then conspiracies of parasitic bankers had throttled normal business processes. Thus Ford could write, "this depression was planned by finance to speculate against all other valuable things." Why, the world was just beginning! The earth was virtually raw materials. Failures to produce, to find employment, could only signal torpor or conspiracy.

Caught in the coils of such thinking, Ford lashed out not only at bankers, but also at all forms of what he regarded as laxity and immorality. For example, jazz and smoking were fostered by outsiders. As the *Dearborn Independent* explained, "A certain stream of nasty Orientalism has been observed in this country to be affecting our literature, our amusements, our social conduct and our business standards. . . ."[27] To ward off this menace, Ford took up the fraudulent *Protocols of the Elders of Zion* and began his crusade in the *Independent.* This campaign cannot be understood as a specifically motivated one. The Jews were an unhappy target, victims chosen somewhat accidentally to exemplify Ford's world view. The attack resulted from the "logic" of Ford's larger vision.

As already noted, Ford inveighed against the international gold conspiracy and the strikes, wars, depressions, and other social problems it fostered. The Jews, rather than representing an independent threat, were but an unfortunate part of his larger obsession. The attacks launched in the *Dearborn Independent* followed the pattern of nineteenth-century attacks on "Popery." Gustavus Meyers finds, in his *History of Bigotry in the United States,* that fears of similar worldwide conspiracies of nefarious enemies, whose machinations had lasted for centuries and threatened the very existence of society, had recurred throughout earlier American history. The *Independent*'s editors were thus able to draw on a long tradition which previously had villified Masons and Catholics. Their rhetoric, however, was also part of a much older tradition, and the *Independent*'s Manichaean world view resembled the myths of demonology, created first by the Catholic Inquisition and later by Protestants. The elaborate mythology they created, as H. R. Trevor-Roper explained in *The European Witch-Craze,* "owes its system entirely to the inquisitors themselves." The pact with the devil, the witch's sabbath, and carnal intercourse with demons were the fabrications of the persecutors, not the persecuted. "Just as the anti-Semites built up, out of disconnected tidbits of scandal, their systematic mythology of ritual murder, poisoned wells, and the world wide conspiracy of the Elders of Zion, so the Hammers of Witches built up their systematic mythology of Satan's kingdom. . . ."[28]

As Trevor-Roper's comparison makes clear, the myths of sixteenth-century witch-hunters provide the pattern for Ford's anti-Semitism, and it should not be surprising to find that there were similarities of doctrine. Ford's was not the Deist god of the eighteenth century, who, after establishing his laws, left the universe to run like a great clock. Ford, like the demonologists, conceived of invisible forces active in the world. That he conceived of good forces has been discussed at length, but it should not be surprising that he saw dark forces as well—an evil world of international conspiracy, strikes, Jews, *Protocols,* Wall Street interests, dupes, socialists, and political stooges.

Certainly this begins to resemble the Puritan imagination, throwing into question the argument that Ford was more analogous to a Platonist, albeit a somewhat muddled and unsystematic one. Here Trevor-Roper's work clarifies Ford's position, for it demonstrates that belief in demonology was as fervid and consistent among Platonists as any other group in Reformation Europe. There is thus no need to enroll Ford as a descendant of Puritan witch-hunters to explain his Manichaean imagination, for his own religious conceptions had demonstrated their compatibility with such ideas and persecutions in previous times.

This is not to doubt the influence of characteristic American perspectives or the possibility that the choice of the Jews as a target stemmed from Populist influences, as Richard Hofstadter proposed. However, he himself admitted that no evidence has been found to directly link Ford and Populist anti-Semitism, or other ideas such as the free coinage of silver and attacks on the gold conspiracy. Even if such an origin could be shown, it would hardly prove that Ford was himself a Populist. As his relationships to Emerson and Jackson make clear, Ford was independent, and even when influenced by others he always drew his own conclusions. As a final note, one of Ford's closest associates remembered that although acquainted with William Jennings Bryan, Ford had little respect for his ideas, and considered Bryan to be "just a politician."

The long pedigree of his prejudice aside, there is no justification for Ford's attitude, and although he made a formal retraction of his attacks on the Jewish people it lost some credibility when he made only token efforts at repairing the damage he had done. The *Independent* articles and the books he had reprinted had been distributed throughout the world and translated into many languages; they had received their credibility from Ford's name. No comparable counter-publicity campaign followed up Ford's retraction, nor did he act to quash further use of *The International Jew*.

Perhaps more convincing indications that Ford's Manichaean perspective was deeply ingrained and basically unaltered was his decision to retain William Cameron, the *Independent* editor officially responsible for the defamation of the Jewish people, and the man who swore under oath that he had done so without Ford's knowledge. Since minor misconduct usually resulted in immediate dismissal at the Rouge, it seems more than plausible that Cameron loyally sacrificed himself in court for his employer's prejudices and was protected in return.

While Ford did speak out in favor of allowing German Jews to emigrate to the United States in 1938, in the same year he accepted the Grand Order of the Great Eagle of Germany, a medal sent by Hitler on the occasion of his seventy-fifth birthday.[29] While Ford's refusal to give up the decoration was perhaps not meant to imply support for the Führer, it hinted that he was at best insensitive to the Jewish plight.

Superficially a discussion of Ford's political and economic ideas leads one to Marx, Jackson, and Hitler. Ford himself was like none of these men, yet his ideas are at times comparable to those of all three. These comparisons would lead to confusion were one to view Ford as a derivative thinker. He was not. His economic ideas were only superficially like those of Marx, who did not influence him. His Jacksonian beliefs led not to the White House but to Muscle Shoals; not to bank abolition, but to a new "energy dollar." His vituperation against the Jews was the rhetoric of a Manichaean imagination, as his belief in parasites and conspiracies was more general than specific. These beliefs, like those in the "energy dollar" and "the wage motive," ultimately sprang from quite another body of ideas that focused on reunifying factory and farm, body and mind, intuition and experience, man and nature. That these ideas in extension could become unfortunate and even dangerous cannot be denied, but to confuse their origins would be to mistake Ford for a Hitler or a Marx. While both comparisons are exciting, they are far less than edifying.

Yet, if Ford was not a Marxist or a Nazi, a Puritan or a Jacksonian, where did his ideas come from, and what was his place in a larger pattern of cultural analysis?

# CHAPTER SIX

# BY INSTINCT AN ENGINEER

*We love characters in proportion as they are impulsive
and  spontaneous. The less a man think or know about
his virtues, the better we like him. . . . only in our easy,
simple spontaneous action are we strong, and by contenting ourselves with obedience we become divine.*
Marked by Henry Ford in "Spiritual Laws"

*An inevitable dualism bisects nature, so that each thing
is a half, and suggests another thing to make it whole.
. . . The same dualism underlies the nature and condition of man. Every excess causes a defect; every defect
an excess. Every sweet hath its sour; every evil its good.*
"Compensation," Ford's favorite Emerson essay

Ford shaped his world far more directly than most men. Wish easily
became fulfillment, perception became reality, as he created new foods,
new forms of transportation, and new methods of production. His
perceptions led directly to action, whether in the form of a Peace Ship
or a meticulous restoration of his parents' home. Ford's intentions
found their fullest expression in later years, when social norms, conventions of taste, and the usual restrictions of inadequate means all
but disappeared. He could buy or build anything; he could, and did,
meet anyone, from Amos 'n Andy, Charles Lindbergh, H. G. Wells,
Charlie Chaplin, and Will Rogers to presidents.

While most people have limited opportunities to grow and change in
later life, Ford's industrial empire forced him to adjust to new conditions.

If he had greater opportunities to transform his world, the relation was reciprocal. The greater the scope of his intentions, the more impact the world might have upon him. The larger Ford's aims, the more vulnerable he became.

Paradoxically, the mind which helped transform the world into one industrial civilization appears to have been too unstructured to accomplish anything, if that mind is mirrored accurately in Ford's interviews and private notebooks. It did not work in either a linear or a cause-and-effect manner, but instead focused entirely on its goals. Ford was liable to follow any chance thought or interruption in his thinking, trusting to intuition. Numerous observers noted his epigrammatic style of conversation, characterized by strange juxtapositions. Similarly, in his notebooks one finds leaps from one topic to the next with no transition or discernible connection.

To read them is rather like looking at a medieval picture, with its apparently arbitrary construction and lack of perspective. Eventually one learns how to "see" such pictures, by adjusting one's categories, giving prominence to figures of spiritual importance regardless of their position in space and time. Similarly, Ford's notebooks move back and forth among unquestioned ends which had the highest priority, unconcerned with traversing the ground between them. Just as the medieval artists assumed an underlying order and harmony moving in the spiritual world, Ford assumed that an underlying intelligence ordered and harmonized his thoughts in accord with a larger plan. A sample notebook entry illustrates both points:

Where does faith come from  answer. Just around the corner; look. Thought and work  application. All trouble comes from idleness  We are all here for experience  War is murder and Thou shall no murder do  greed and power is the cause of most all trouble If you truely ask to be Guided  you will be led in every move you make

The final sentence suggests why Emerson's statement "only in our easy, simple, spontaneous action are we strong," appealed to Ford. His action mirrored his thought, in all its apparent contradictions, inexplicable reversals, and startling transitions. Nor should we miss the second part of Emerson's statement that "by contenting ourselves with obedience we become divine." Here obedience and spontaneity are identified, and unpremeditated action becomes equated with divinity. Ford could justify personal inclination as his impulsive expression of a harmonious relationship with the cosmos.

Such obedience did not bring with it a duty to other men, but rather to the power of the Universal Brain, to the underlying direction of history, to the enigma of electricity, and to the forces which could recreate the raw materials of the earth. When Ford wrote in his notebook "Our spontaneous is always the best,"[1] he was thus announcing a relationship to the world untrammeled by the needs of his fellow men.

Ford's Emersonian sense of independence and self-reliance had its origin in youth. The conventional explanation, recounted in popular biographies, is that Ford rebelled against his father and went on his own as a mechanic. More recently, on discovering this story was untrue, Anne Jardim has argued in a Freudian study that Ford had a "need to create a harsh punitive father where none existed." But the myth of Ford's rebellion was perpetuated by the public. He did not repeat the myth to his immediate family, nor to Anne Hood, who interviewed him for the Greenfield Village school newspaper. She reported, "William Ford was a kind and just father, interested in his son, but he was a man of few words"; a terse but accurate account of their relationship. Ford clearly said nothing against his father to either Anne Hood or his sister, Mrs. Edsel Ford Ruddiman, who was interviewed years later.[2] The currency of stories which tell of Ford's youthful rebellion reflects the tendency to pour his life into a familiar mold. Ford could no more have changed them than he could have convinced the American public of reincarnation.

What sort of man was William Ford? This question will prove far more fruitful than speculation about possible conflicts with his son. He was an adventurous man who had left Ireland when a youth; a man "handy with tools," who also bought the latest farm equipment as it appeared; a man interested in advances in technology, who traveled to the Philadelphia Exposition in 1876; a reader of the philosophy of Herbert Spencer, whose books stood in the family room of his home; and a man who was sent by his neighbors, along with several others, to study the possible adoption of electric cars like those operating in Cleveland. His group reported favorably on the cars.

These facts suggest that William Ford was not a narrow farmer, but a man open to new ideas, as in Spencer, and new technologies, both in agriculture and elsewhere. His committee's decision to eliminate horse-drawn cars on Michigan Avenue suggests that he was not a traditionalist, and after his visit to Philadelphia he "and his friends constantly speculated upon what this was to mean to the average farmer. . . . An imaginative boy with a mechanical bent who heard these speculations was impressed."

Thus, whether young Henry ultimately rebelled against his father is, in a sense, beside the point. William Ford's household provided an atmosphere where technological innovations were discussed. His father was not entirely provincial, for he had emigrated from Ireland and visited Philadelphia and Cleveland. Also as the reading in Spencer should suggest, William Ford gave his son a very unprejudiced attitude toward religion. William Ford hung the Masonic emblem in their family room,[3] and Henry also became a member, later reaching the thirty-third (and highest) degree. This common interest again suggests that father and son were compatible and shared many interests, not the least of which was a concern with machinery.

In fact, Henry first worked for the James Flowers Brothers Machine Shop, whose owner regularly visited the Ford home. Whether William Ford arranged with Mr. Flowers to hire his mechanically minded son or not, one may discern his influence on Henry's interests, religious opinions, and early employment. The accounts of a young boy running away from home, far from being Ford's view of his relationship with his father, were fabricated by biographers using a formula that Henry could never have escaped, but one which he cannily realized would create free publicity.

While Ford's relationship to his father was important, his mother assumed a larger place in his imagination. She was "responsible, religious, interested in reading," and diligent. A stickler for cleanliness and proper diet, she prompted her son's strictness in the same matters. Her daughter recalled, "Mother was an energetic person. When there was a job to do it was done quickly and well."

But beyond these habits, which Henry acquired, Mary Ford had an intuitive grasp of her son's personality. As he later reminisced, "She read what was in my mind. . . . It was a way she had. I understand it better now, for I've done it myself many times." Ford's belief in thought transference and precognition stemmed from these early experiences. Like his mother, he claimed, "I've answered questions before they were asked; I've seen people approaching me and known before they reached me what they were going to propose."[4] Because Ford believed he had

shared this ability with his mother, precognition seemed perfectly
natural to him.

Ford also may have relied upon dreams to guide him in decisions.
He once told Allan Benson that he had a recurrent dream before each
new business venture, but when pressed for details, he refused to say
more. In another interview he once said that "The subconscious mind
is charged with many memories that we have apparently forgotten. It
takes an arousing experience of some sort to bring scenes from the deeps
where they slumber to the surface of consciousness." Perhaps dreams
were the medium which he believed expressed experiences of other
lives. If so, however, there is no record of Ford's dreams, and only one
reference to dreams appears in his notebooks—"Life is a dream"—and
that may be a song title.[5]

Ford sometimes referred to his mother in later years as "the believer,"
and characterized his wife in the same way. Both women encouraged
the independent and intuitive side of his nature, while his father shared
with Ford an openness to technological change. And it was in machinery that Ford's intuitive nature first sought expression, as his mother
encouraged him. He fondly remembered that his first "steam engine"
had been a sled carrying a teakettle from her kitchen, and later had
the scene painted by Irving Bacon. At seven he saw his first watch,
owned by a German farmhand, and by age twelve he could often be
found "gazing fondly into a jeweler's window" in Detroit.

In that same year he saw a steam engine that traveled on back roads
under its own power. Years later he would pencil in his jotbook "In
july 1876 The first portable engine came. . . . That showed me that
I was by instinct an Engineer." The full significance of that event,
however, can only be realized when placed in chronological sequence.
Previous biographers seldom have seen the context of this important
encounter. But a few months earlier Henry's mother, Mary Ford, died
in childbirth, on March 29, 1876. At thirteen, Ford took this sudden
death hard. Years later he told Edgar Guest that he "thought a great
wrong had been done to me,"[6] and that it took him years before he
was reconciled to her passing.

The strength of this attachment is revealed by his careful restoration
of their home as it had existed in 1876. Ford searched nationwide for
the kitchen stove, whose serial number he had remembered. The yard
was carefully excavated to discover fragments of the original dishes.
Family furnishings were regathered or accurately replaced. An exact

duplicate of the living room rug was located and its owner convinced to sell it. Once the house was renovated, Ford and his wife, Clara, spent occasional afternoons there with the family. The house was one of the last moved to Greenfield Village, and it stood on its original site for virtually all of Ford's life.

This restoration suggests how difficult her death was for him. His love and the intuitive relationship he shared with her had to find other outlets. When the road steam engine appeared three months after Mary Ford's death and young Henry suddenly discovered himself "by instinct an Engineer" he was transforming and redirecting his emotional life. Where previously he had intuited his mother's thoughts, now he would direct that intuition towards machinery. Later, the precognition he had shared with her would be turned toward industrial trends—the universal car, mass production, the Five Dollar Day, the five-day week.

Ford's first sight of the moving road steam engine may of course be taken as a glimpse of the possibility of mechanized road transportation. However, it was not his first view of a steam engine, nor was he ignorant of the existence of road engines. Henry had been in Detroit machine shops on earlier occasions, and at seven had had a steam engine explained to him. The impact of the experience with the road engine must be attributed to other causes. The road engine hardly would have been etched in Ford's mind if he had not been seeking an outlet for the feelings he had for his so recently departed mother. He could "remember that engine as though I had seen it only yesterday...," even to its revolutions per minute, horsepower, and the name of the operator.

Ford's mother had always encouraged his mechanical interests. In one early schoolyard experiment, Henry and friends constructed a water-wheel. It worked well, but the dam backed water up into a farmer's fields. Ford also supervised the construction of a forge, foraging coal from along the railroad tracks, and melting together in an iron ladle "all the pieces of tin and brass and lead" he could find. An even more ambitious experiment was the construction of a steam turbine. Because Mary Ford encouraged these interests, her memory may have become intertwined with these interests. After her death, Henry sensed her passing in mechanical terms. As his sister recalled, he likened the house after her death to a "watch without its mainspring."[7] He had lost his impetus, and the rhythm and order of his life were disrupted. For the next three years he tinkered, made castings, patterns, and parts for some farm equipment. He grew restless, convinced that the mainspring

of his life now lay in the machine shops of Detroit, where he went to
work in 1879.

In Detroit young Henry served what might be called an apprenticeship in various machine shops, worked with a jeweler, and eventually
became an engineer with the Detroit Edison Electric Company. He
brought to these jobs the adventurousness, manual skill, and keen
interest in technology that he had shared with his father. He pursued
them with the energy, diligence, and independence of his mother.
He was apparently not concerned much with religious questions,
but was open to rapid advances in technology. By the time he began
serious work on his automobile, Ford had the exacting precision of
the watchmaker, the knowledge of metals and steam power of an engineer, and an extensive experience with electricity.

Perhaps as important as these abilities, however, were the friends he
made in the various shops and businesses of Detroit. He would later
draw on both their technical skills and their financial resources. Ford
was not a solitary recluse during these years. He had many friends and
learned a great deal from them. For example, in 1880 a fellow worker
at the Detroit Dry Dock Engine Works showed him an article on the
invention of the internal combustion engine by Dr. Nicolas Otto in
Germany.[8] Ford was soon reading the technical magazines of the day.

For the next eleven years Ford was not settled, even after his
marriage to Clara Bryant in 1888. He worked at a number of jobs,
each with some success, but left them all. He also gave up his option of
carrying on the family farm, preferring jobs which taught him about
machines, including an Otto gas engine he repaired in 1885. Ford's automobile business did not logically evolve from this job, however, and
it appears he even considered mass production of watches for a few
years. When he permanently settled in Detroit late in 1891 as an engineer for Detroit Edison, however, Ford had begun to focus his energies
on making an automobile.

He became close friends with a successful inventor, Charles B. King,
who had made the first automobile in Detroit, and who gave Ford some
of the parts used in his first car. Years later King made a search for the
original house at 58 Bagby Street where the first Ford had been made, a
building Ford believed had been torn down, and discovered it behind a
storefront. That discovery and other unusual events are recorded in a
little-known work that King had privately printed, *Psychic Reminiscences,*

which describes "incidents which seem beyond analysis from a materialist's point of view." Like Ford, King felt that "Confidence is a beacon that leads far, Fear, its opposite, is a deterrent." King felt that inventions sprang from the "immortal mind," that "all things are possible," and that men "must always carry that thought of no limitation to our latent power," if they were to carry out their most ambitious ideas. To a struggling young mechanic like Ford, the belief that his acts were part of a plan "preconceived by Immortal Mind" must have come as a welcome boon during the long hours of tinkering, the financial depression of the 1890's, and the successive formation and dissolution of his first automobile companies.

Rejecting Calvinism, which made no provision for man's limitless powers, and the eighteenth-century conception of natural laws, which virtually eliminated an "immortal brain," Ford believed creation was a partnership between man and God—a relation not so much dialectical as transcendental. In one of his notebooks Ford wrote, "God needed Edison."[9] These three words contain much of his philosophy. Ford's deity had preconceived the universe, but needed particular men open to his influence to carry out the "immortal plan"—men such as Edison, whom Ford heard of "during 1879 or '80 when the invention and quick adoption of his incandescent light made him a world figure. . . ." It may not be accidental that when Ford left the farm for the last time he took a job with the Detroit Edison Company. That employment eventually led to a meeting with Edison, when Ford attended the company's annual convention in August 1896, accompanying Alexander Dow, president of the Detroit branch.

Years later Ford recalled that first meeting in his *Edison as I Knew Him.* At a dinner when the possible expansion of the company into electric carriages was discussed, Dow turned the conversation to Ford, gesturing towards him and saying, "There's a young fellow who has made a gas car." Immediately Edison had Ford moved to the chair beside him and asked numerous questions, while Ford sketched his work. Then, as he recalled,

When I had finished, he brought his fist down on the table with a bang, and said:
"Young man, that's the thing; you have it. Keep at it. Electric cars must keep near to power stations. The storage battery is too heavy. Steam cars won't do either. . . ."
That bang on the table was worth worlds to me. No man up to then had given me any encouragement.

That encounter spurred Ford to work harder, since he believed that "Edison was already . . . the greatest man in the world."

Edison was the most prolific inventor of his times, and in later life Ford attributed this to two sources: Edison's natural talent inherited from previous incarnations, and his capacity for hard work. He became a model for the younger Ford. The following words might describe either man; they are Ford's.

Edison has a wonderfully imaginative mind and also a most remarkable memory. Yet all of his talents would never have brought anything big into the world had he not had within him that driving force which pushes him on . . . until he has finished. . . . He will not recognize even the possibility of defeat. He believes that unflinching, unremitting work will accomplish anything. It was this genius for hard work that fired me as a lad and made Mr. Edison my hero. . . .[10]

That Edison also rejected conventional religion, came from a small Michigan town, had very limited schooling, and received much of his early training and self-confidence from his mother, made the sympathies between the two men very strong.

After meeting Edison, Ford worked much harder than before, until he quit his job and in 1899 formed his first motor car company. Ford never doubted the future of the motor car, and generally drew all those around him into his own project. This was more than a matter of his enthusiasm. Ford apparently had a magnetic personality, and others were drawn to work with him. As Olson found in his research; "He could talk other men into helping him, backing him, working for him. . . ." Time and again in the remarks of interviewers and in the reminiscences of Ford workers one finds attempts to define Ford's personal quality as "charm," "magnetism," "naturalness," and so on.

Ford had been a leader among his school fellows as early as 1876, yet the force of character he later developed was not simply an extension of his role in the rural playground. Ford attained more than a personal charm; he achieved a self-possession, a self-assurance that other men found attractive and were willing to obey. Ford's magnetism (for want of a better word) did not rely upon any social graces or affectations. Not one interviewer ever came away with the impression that Ford was anything but direct, and he was often called childlike in his simplicity.

Without classifying the particular quality which gave Ford his hold over other men, one can discover when it became noticeable to others around him, and see what other events occurred at the same time. While his character did not change suddenly, it was transformed between the time he ran a sawmill and lived in Dearborn and the period fifteen years later when he rapidly expanded the Ford Motor Company. Certainly the personal contact with Edison about halfway through this period was crucial in developing Ford's self-confidence, inspiring him to work even harder on his gas buggy. And yet, even after that meeting and the successful construction of his second car, Ford did not move decisively. Two early Ford companies were formed and dissolved, and although the reasons for these failures are not clear, and certainly stemmed in part from difficulties with some of the investors, Ford's drive and personal magnetism simply were not yet in evidence.

In these first companies Ford worked secretly at times, and focused much attention on developing racing cars, partly to increase public confidence in his abilities. Commercial production never developed, and while some dispute about how many cars his Detroit Automobile Company made, even the highest estimates are less than thirty in a two-year period. As Nevins and Hill summarize:

During the year 1900 the Detroit Automobile Company ground slowly to a stop. *Probably* the machine it could make was not good enough, and was too expensive. Ford explained later that the car would not sell. *Apparently* he wanted to make a better one, and his stockholders vetoed the idea [emphasis added].

As the italicized words suggest, information about the reasons for the company's failure is incomplete. Yet had the Ford personality of 1914 been involved, a clear conflict between Ford and his stockholders would have developed; he would not simply have accepted a veto. Nor would that later Ford have made a machine which "probably was not good enough," or one that "would not sell." These explanations for the company's failure, because of a poor product or because Ford did not press hard enough for his ideas, simply do not fit well with the Ford who emerged a few years later.

In 1901 Ford was thirty-eight years old. It had been five years since Edison encouraged him and several years had passed since he had left his job with Detroit Edison. It was a crucial year. While he had retained the confidence of some potential backers, the successful racer was essential. What were the circumstances surrounding Ford's success?

An apparently minor event in January of that year must not be over-looked. Henry, Clara, and Edsel moved in with William Ford to economize, although they were well enough off to lend $200 to his brother John in February.[11] These events indicate an amiable relation between father and son and show that Ford maintained a continuing interest in his family. His thoughts may also have returned to his long-deceased mother, now that he lived with his father again under the same roof.

In this year, when Ford was brought into closer contact with his family and his success hung in the balance, he also adopted the belief in reincarnation. A fellow engineer, Oliver E. Barthel (whom Ford would persuade to work for him in the following months), lent him *A Short View of Great Questions* by Major Orlando Smith, which was found fifty years later among the Ford papers at his Fairlane Estate. Barthel lent Ford the work the day of President McKinley's funeral, and numerous long talks on religion followed. As Ford later remembered, "I got the idea [reincarnation] from a book by Orlando Smith. Until I discovered this theory I was unsettled. . . . When I discovered reincarnation it was as if I had found a universal plan."[12]

Reincarnation carried with it the belief that one's past experiences were not entirely lost upon birth. As Ford later said in his work on Edison, reincarnation led directly to the Model T.

A man comes into this world, I believe, with accumulated experiences which make his mind into a certain sort of career. My first car was a part of that experience and it had run. From it I learned some facts which I was putting into my second car. . . . The process is still going on. . . .

After 1901 Ford viewed his life as a part of a much longer process, and all work became meaningful even if he did not always know why. "Work is futile if we cannot utilize the experience we collect in one life in the next." The futility which Ford may have occasionally felt during his first thirty-eight years was erased. Where before he had been worried about having time enough (and had once wished to mass produce watches, for that matter), now he "realized that there was a chance to work out my ideas. Time was no longer limited. I was no longer a slave to the hands of the clock. There was time enough to plan and to create."

His earlier life Ford now saw as a great preparation, and although he was nearing forty, his relative economic insecurity no longer seemed important. He left behind him an unsettled early life, and now found "the calmness that the long view of life gives to us."[13] One distress of early life effectively calmed was the loss of his mother. Where earlier he had felt that "a great wrong had been done to me," now he could view her abbreviated life as part of a larger series of lives. Thus, to the suggestion that if she had lived longer, Ford could have made her very happy, Ford responded in 1924 that he had "thought of that too; but I believe now it is better as it is. I believe her work here was finished. She had done all she could do for us and she was called away."

Through his new belief Ford was reconciled to both the loss of his mother and to the slow pace of his early development. He no longer felt driven by the hands of the clock. His sense of time had altered, and with a new, long view of his existence came both a great calmness and a tremendous self-assurance, expressed as personal magnetism which drew others to him. Barthel later remembered his surprise at Ford's strong interest in Smith's work, and concluded, "I think at that time Mr. Ford had some form of intuitive relationship, or he felt that he was in tune with the infinite." Barthel's words suggest that Ford's acceptance of reincarnation may have been antedated by other beliefs or experiences which he could not understand, but which had led him to the conviction that he was "in tune with" forces outside himself.

Although Emerson would appear a possible source for such a belief, Barthel declared that "This was before Emerson entered his life at all." In fact, Ford was probably led to Emerson by Smith, who quotes him at several points, including a passage from "Compensation," later Ford's favorite essay.[14] Reading appears to have followed and clarified early experience, so that in middle age Ford's life suddenly entered a new stage. Students of American culture are familiar with this pattern from the lives of Whitman and Melville. With Ford there was no literary manifestation of the change such as *Leaves of Grass,* nor did he say, with Melville, that he could date his life from his twenty-fifth year.[15] But just as Whitman had been one of a hundred New York journalists until Emerson brought him to a boil, Ford was but one of a hundred tinkerers until he found a way to organize his creative energies, and simultaneously to find a pattern in his previous life. As he said in 1928:

I was forty when I went into business, forty when I began to evolve the

Ford plant. But all the time I was getting ready. That is one thing the larger view does for you, it enables you to take time to get ready. Most of my life has been spent in preparation. . . .[16]

Ironically, of course, Ford had not possessed this "larger view" during his time of preparation, and rather than lengthening his period of "getting ready" the belief in reincarnation came at the decisive moment, giving him the confidence and the self-assurance he would need to succeed. In the following two years he constructed his racer, found backing for the Ford Motor Company, and began successful production. Within two more years he gained control by forcing a major partner, Malcolmson, out of the business, and, soon after, against the objections of his other stockholders, he began work on the universal cheap car. Thus "the calmness that the long view of life gives to us," served as the catalyst for his intense activities and unswerving purpose of the following years. Freed from self-doubt, released from responsibility for his actions, assured of his hunches by reincarnated knowledge and precognition, he now knew why only his easy and natural actions were strong. And in proportion as his character became impulsive and spontaneous, he would engage the American public.

# CHAPTER SEVEN

# THE WATCH'S MAINSPRING

Ford's encounter with the theory of reincarnation spurred his development as an industrialist and also encouraged him to expand his ideas. In the turbulent years that followed he also found time to read a good deal, or had Clara read to him. John Burroughs felt that "Ford was the real thing, a man of sterling quality" but "crude in his philosophy" because "His philosophical ideas were those of a man who turned his attention in that direction late in life." Burroughs himself had a good bit to do with the "turning," as he learned from Clara Ford: ". . . by chance he had read one of my books and enjoyed it so much that his wife bought him a full set. She said the books had quite a marked effect on his attitude of mind." In fact, Burroughs "started new currents in him that stuck by him. . .and he was no longer utterly absorbed in his car."[1]

Through the naturalist Ford became intrigued with Henry David Thoreau and Emerson, so much so that in the midst of creating the assembly line they made a pilgrimage to Concord together, where they were guided around Walden by Emerson's friend and biographer, Frank Sanborn. Ford's reading in transcendentalism abetted his interest in things outside his factory, and despite his age—fifty in 1913—he began a period of rapid development. Contrary to the Jardim thesis, Ford was hardly static in later life. One intimate reminisced, "He learned very quickly. You didn't have to tell him much or show him." Will Rogers, who knew him only in later life, found Ford "easy to talk to and interested in everything." One former employee believed that Ford's greatest learning period came between the ages of fifty-five and sixty-eight.[2] Slowly weaned from his sole interest in business, he created a world view centered upon reincarnation and supplemented by Emerson, Burroughs, and Thoreau. It bore some resemblance to Christian Science and New Thought, but was not inspired by them.

The pieces of this world view fell into place quickly after the assembly line was in successful operation, and bore first fruit in the announcement of the Five Dollar Day in 1914. By 1916 he had begun the search for gasoline substitutes, completed the basic outlines of what would be chemurgy, and manifested an interest in plastics and lighter materials. He acquired much of his anti-Semitic bias in 1915 while on the Peace Ship. On board, Ford was away from his family and business for the first extended period, and he came into contact with many pacifists and other thinkers, as the delegates held numerous meetings and debates.

Apparently during this trip he learned of the *Protocols of Zion* and began to link capitalism and the Jewish people with wars and revolutions. Earlier Ford had picked up some Darwinian theory, which he lectured at a reporter from the *New York Herald* almost a year before the Peace Ship. The reporter concluded Ford "evidently believes that there is a chance that the superman may come after us." However, Ford may not have known Nietzsche's name, much less his philosophy, and the "superman" referred to was probably akin to an idea of Edison's that men would eventually evolve who would need no sleep, or to Ford's own notion that with proper diet one could easily live and be productive until the age of one hundred.

Another revealing remark came in the same interview. "'Emerson said,' went on Mr. Ford, 'that the chief want in life is somebody to make us do what we can do.'"[3] Although he seems to have misconstrued Emerson, clearly a new impulse had awakened in Ford, the desire to reform and direct others. But as his aims broadened, so did the public interest focused upon him. When his philosophy merged with his ability to act on a chance thought, Ford would prove especially vulnerable to ridicule.

Even the Five Dollar Day was roundly attacked in some quarters, not to mention some of the later exploits like the Peace Ship. Yet initially Ford withstood criticism, confident that he was right in his decisions, reenforced by the success of the Model T and the high wage policy. He even made a point to read criticism. An editor who worked briefly for him, reported in 1920 that he had "seen him read through a column of bitter denunciation without wincing, pick out a single line, and remark, 'They are right in this. They have got it on us there; let's correct that.' I have seen him read through bales of clippings criticizing him seemingly without affecting him." Ford's interest in criticism should not be viewed as either a taste for self-torture or a sign that he felt so secure no criticism could touch him. One of Ford's strengths was the ability to learn from mistakes and failings. Before 1920 he was open to the need for improvements in his business and his personal life, although this flexibility did not extend to changes suggested in the Model T.

One source for Ford's interest in the criticism of others lay in his favorite Emerson essay, "Compensation," where he marked the following, "The wise man throws himself on the side of his assailants. It is more his interest than theirs to find his weak point."[4] As long as Ford maintained this attitude, his mind continued to expand, assimilating new ideas and remaining flexible. Yet as early as 1912 there were warning signals that he would not tolerate some criticism. That year he and Clara went to Europe, and some of his engineers designed an improved Model T to surprise him on his return.

Instead of praising their work and energy, however, Ford angrily had the prototype demolished. The outburst was a sign that beneath Ford's genial surface flowed an undercurrent of quite a different sort, one which could be fed by his education. Belief in Darwinian ideas, his understanding from Emerson that men chiefly needed "somebody to make us do what we can do," and a fear of the Jewish people were all explosive ingredients. Each tended to reenforce Ford's sense of his own separation from others and his superiority, whether through evolution, leadership ability, or race. Thus there would clearly be limits to the "assailants" Ford would tolerate or change sides for.

Unfortunately, Ford's toleration was battered by a series of newspaper attacks and courtroom humiliations, beginning with the Peace Ship and abating in 1919 after the *Chicago Tribune* suit. The press's failure to take his Peace Ship seriously was followed by jeers when he reversed himself and began war production. Then the armistice drew near, Ford lost an important suit to the Dodge Brothers, and he was forced to pay larger dividends than he wished to at a time of expansion. But the Mt. Clemens trial was certainly the greatest humiliation, and for the rest of his life Ford was willing to go to great lengths to avoid further courtroom appearances.

While this libel suit endeared Ford to the great mass of Americans, a fact which he quickly grasped, he believed that parasites and conspirators were attacking him. The *Chicago Tribune* lawsuit was only his first assault in what was a general attack on a corrupt system. His weapons were varied, including Muscle Shoals, the energy dollar, and purchase of the *Dearborn Independent,* to provide him with his own press. Within the plant his attack focused on executives who would not blindly obey his orders, leading to the firing or resignation of many fine executives. His major personal defense would be an increasing isolation, until by the early 1920's Dean Marquis concluded that his mind was about as isolated as it possibly could be.[5]

Before this self-imposed isolation began Ford had already been extremely independent. He had set himself apart by his insistence on playing his "hunches," whether they led to the universal car or universal peace on the *Oscar II;* his trial-and-error methods; his attempts to do the difficult or supposedly impossible; and his tenacity. Once isolated, his ideas did not change, but his espousal of them began to take new forms. Where earlier his faith in intuition had manifested itself constructively in the face of a general public indifference to the horseless carriage, now he refused to allow anyone to question his judgment. He would deny the public's demands for a new car in the late 1920's, when his obstinacy would continue until declining sales forced him to close the factory for a year. Increasingly, when Ford met opposition, he expressed his ideas in a hostile or even destructive way, until it appeared to some observers that he had two separate natures.

Louis Lochner, who knew Ford intimately during the Peace Ship's voyage and stay in Scandinavia, observed,

Take any recent front-page picture or photograph of Henry Ford, and lay a sheet of paper on top . . . to cover one eye and one-half of his face. You will find that the left half is the face of the idealist, the dreamer, the humanitarian. Kindliness and good-will beam forth from the eye. There is something gentle about the expression. You are attracted at once to the man.

Then take the other half. It is the shrewd face of a sharp business man, alert, somewhat suspicious, somewhat cynical, full of cunning. The spiritual quality of the left eye gives place to a calculating materialism in the right.

Lochner believed these physical differences mirrored Ford's inner makeup; he was a man of vastly different moods. It was the humanitarian who had left his business to sail to Norway, but after lying sick for a short period in a hotel, it was the "somewhat cynical" Ford who slipped hastily out of the hotel without even saying goodbye. Lochner, like so many others who were intimate with Ford, refused to believe that Ford alone had decided to do such a thing, blaming the sudden change in attitude on Dean Marquis.

Marquis himself was not immune to Ford's sudden changes in mood. The mind which had always hurtled from one thought to the next, with no apparent connection, allowed emotions to do the same. And just as Ford's ideas seldom seemed part of a larger pattern, his emotions seemed similarly unaccountable. Marquis had a chance to observe Ford closely while he managed the short-lived Sociological Department, a product of Ford's interest in the welfare of workers. Marquis was also well-acquainted with Mrs. Ford, who sent him to Norway with instructions to get Henry back home as soon as possible, with or without peace. Marquis was soon to leave the Ford Company, however, after he learned that Ford's benign surface concealed other traits which he could not accept. His effort to understand his former employer resulted in *Henry Ford, An Interpretation,* and the book apparently struck a sensitive spot, for Ford tried to suppress it by buying as many copies as possible. He would not throw himself on the side of this assailant.

The Marquis portrait parallels Lochner's, and goes even farther. Instead of Lochner's static observation of Ford's profiles, Marquis discovered a dynamic expression of Ford's moods in his whole physique.

These variations in mental moods . . . are generally accompanied by outward changes in physical appearance. Today he stands erect, lithe, agile, full of life, happy as a child . . . But tomorrow . . . He will have the appearance of a man shrunken by long illness. The shoulders droop, and there is a forward slant to the body . . . His face is deeply lined . . . There is a light in the eye that reveals a fire burning within. . . .

Or, as Allan Benson described the same phenomenon:

It is the boyish, smiling, youthful Ford that enters the office. In ten seconds, and for no apparent reason, the smile may flit from his face and you behold a man, who, from his eyes up, seems as old as the pyramids. Many little wrinkles dart sidewise from his eyes. The skin is stretched rather tightly over his brow and on each temple is a little vein resembling a blue corkscrew.

These extraordinary descriptions may be compared with Lochner's declaration that "As is his picture, so is Henry Ford: in no other person have I observed so pronounced a dual nature as in my former chief. There seems to be a constant struggle for control on the part of these two natures." Marquis added that Ford seemed caught "in a conflict that at times makes one feel that two personalities are striving within him for mastery."[6] However, while there were two different sides to Ford, it does not necessarily follow that they were struggling for mastery.

Ford's personality was well adapted both to his philosophical views and to his position. He had a philosophical basis for the way he acted, believing himself to be the agent of unseen guiding forces. Whether benign or for the moment malicious, he was but acting out his spontaneous impulses. Nor could one expect him to act kindly towards those he considered parasites, greedy capitalists, or threats to his business. As John Burroughs found, "I never heard any one else abuse the capitalists as he does. He howls against them as bad as any anarchist." But this observation was immediately followed by paradox—"He has a sweet nature, and nobody who's personally acquainted with him can help liking him."

Benson had discovered precisely the same paradox. Ford gave him the *Dearborn Independent* articles attacking the Jews, after Benson declared he "did not share his views. . . . One evening, the subject came up again, and when I expressed the usual dissent he [Ford] asked me if I had read the books he gave me. . . ." When Ford learned Benson hadn't read them he replied, "Well, read them right away. . . . and then if you do not agree with me, don't ever come to see me again." Benson was astounded at this reply, and changed the subject. A few minutes later, Ford apologized, saying, "You can always come here to see me any time you want to."

This incident from the early 1920's illustrates both Ford's dogmatism and willingness to admit a mistake. Unfortunately, in later life Ford had less contact with men like Benson who might draw attention to an error, of etiquette or prejudice. Ford stopped the anti-Jewish articles for a few days after his conversation with Benson because he thought there was "too much anti-Semitic feeling." But increasingly one could only like Ford on his own terms. As one intimate observed, "Mr. Ford was not a man who was inclined to argue about things,"[7] quite possibly because he did not argue things out for himself.

He was not introspective. He intuited, then acted. There were few checks on his will. And if he contradicted himself, then he contradicted himself.

As one *New Republic* reporter presciently observed, it seemed Ford had never felt guilty. His mind was never clouded by self-doubt or an attempt to be consistent in his actions. He did not care what others thought of him, and thus could support peace and shortly afterwards make war material; attack the Jews and then apologize; or insist on a car design and then change his mind the next day.

As J. L. McCloud later reminisced, "He was so completely confident in himself that there was no occasion to worry. . . . best evidence of that was the period when the Model A was being redesigned." In fact, Ford's favorite cartoon came from the period when he closed his factory. In the drawing, Ford stands in the middle of a narrow road surrounded by automobile parts which prevent other motorists, representing his competitors, from passing him. Ford liked this cartoon so much he had it framed and hung in the office.[8]

During this period of serene self-confidence Ford reenforced his beliefs through reading such works as *Reincarnation and the Law of Karma, Reincarnation: Its Necessity, Reincarnation or Immortality?* and *Sacred Book of the Dead, Hindu Spiritualism, Soul Transition and Soul Reincarnation.* He kept his assistant secretary, Frank Campsall, busy writing letters to the Yogi Publishing Society or ordering extra copies of works, which he handed out to visitors. His favorite author was a latter-day member of the New Thought movement, Ralph Waldo Trine, whose *In Tune with the Infinite* he once sent to Douglas Fairbanks as an aid to making a difficult film. In the late 1920's Ford and Trine collaborated on *The Power That Wins,* a dialogue on many subjects, in which Ford affirms his belief in the existence of "little entities" which a man attracted to himself—"invisible lives that are building him up."

When Trine replied by telling the famous story of Swedenborg's vision of the Stockholm fire, Ford answered that the mystic "just happened to be one of those men who can send and receive the intelligent entities that comprised himself. I have seen somewhat similar occurrences"; he concluded that "There is nothing to me that is more thoroughly established than thought transference,"[9] a belief he shared with Thomas Edison. First-hand experience, historical precedent, and intellectual authority all supported Ford's belief in intuitive knowledge.

He also became acquainted with European psychology through a column in the *Detroit Free Press* by C. J. Armstrong, which appeared in 1927 and ran for several years. Ford had his secretary keep a complete set of these articles in scrapbooks, where he read of Dr. Josef Breuer's experiments in hypnosis and their influence on Sigmund Freud, or of the psychology of Alfred Adler. Through reading these daily articles, Ford learned of the theory of the unconscious, the Oedipus complex, and much else.[10] But while they interested him, they did not alter his belief in reincarnation, which he reiterated to Trine two years after the column began.

Ford also shared his thoughts with Murshid Inayat Khan, an Indian mystic who came to Detroit in 1926 to lecture. The two men talked for an hour in the factory library, as Ford reiterated his beliefs in invisible entities, reincarnation, and the importance of religion: "I struggled for many years to solve the problem of religion. . . . I found, as you [Khan] have said, that if I quietly withdrew from the nervous anxiety over things, inventions and the business that drives from every side, there was a renewal of strength in the thought of being a part of the unseen power. . . ." However, Ford did not seem to endorse meditation for its own sake, because "if one meditates too much there is not likely to be much work done."[11]

While these thoughts were reported in the *Detroit News,* no other papers picked up the story. Few wished to see Ford in this light. In contrast many of Ford's chance remarks—such as "history is bunk" which he said but once—were endlessly repeated and are still remembered today. Ford's attempts to communicate with the public were thus distorted both by the selective reporting of the press and the predisposition of the public to accept only certain kinds of information. Ford was surrounded by reporters and staff members who did not understand his ideas. Together they often smoothed over "rough" spots in interviews or removed controversial material altogether, until much of what Ford meant as a challenge was transformed by deletions and rewordings into what the public wanted: self-confirmation, both in their view of Ford and of themselves. One veteran of his news conferences summarized the procedure:

Occasionally, when Ford was in an outlandish mood and saying things which did not square with known fact, a listener at one side of the room would hunch forward and slip into the conversation, "What Mr. Ford meant is—" William J. Cameron, Ford editor, would say, and proceed to file down the edges and touch up the cadence with an adroit carpentry.

Another sub-editor had a different approach. When Ford was lost in an undertow, and no one but him was quite sure what he was driving at, Fred L. Black would remark: "You see, Mr. Ford often speaks in parables," and he would point to the particular parable at bat at the moment. . . .

Ford's lieutenants were determined to keep Ford from making damaging statements; their work helped obscure his ideas sufficiently to make him an ambiguous figure. Ford did not speak in parables or lose his mind in an undertow; his audience preferred to believe that he did. The other executives were just as uncomprehending. Marquis offered an unwitting illustration of their predisposition to dismiss Ford's nonindustrial ideas, and also provides a summary of a number of them.

He speaks at times with the air of great finality, as a man who has received a revelation or has secret sources of information on the great subjects of the day. He talks in short, broken, disconnected sentences. And he has a way of discoursing on one of his favorite themes—Wall Street, the Jew, international bankers . . . world peace through farm tractors and water power, the synthetic cow—in a way that produces among his listeners a profound and embarrassing silence. . . .

The embarrassment of Ford's executives might be compared with their reaction to his lunches of roadside greens. Ford's opinions seemed odd, perhaps even dangerous, certainly ridiculous. None grasped even the possibility that Ford's ideas might have been interconnected. For example, Marquis himself, although a minister, refused to give any importance to Ford's religious ideas. He merely reported, rather stiffly, ". . . Mr. Ford believes, or once did believe, in reincarnation. I have never gone into the subject with him."[12] In other words, not only did the general public, the press, and Ford's fellow executives ignore Ford's unorthodox beliefs, but Marquis, his close friend and advisor from the advent of the Five Dollar Day until the early 1920's, did so as well. Ironically, he declared Ford's mind to be isolated, while intensifying that condition. Marquis's attitude reflects the public's extreme reluctance to inquire into, much less ponder, Ford's philosophical and religious ideas.

Public incomprehension and the ridicule of the years from 1915 until the *Chicago Tribune* suit took their toll. Withdrawn behind a wall of advisors and in sole command of his company after he bought out the other stockholders, Ford began to acquire subsidiary industries, which would ensure his independence. He bought coal mines, forests, ships, a railroad, eventually even a rubber plantation. Simultaneously, he opened his attack on the Jews, and bid for Muscle Shoals. All these activities were marked by fear of outside interference and by a desire to withdraw behind a massive organization, but one which also might expand to embrace the globe. These impulses reflected the dichotomy in Ford's character and were sanctioned by his philosophy. A clergyman who was intimate with Ford recalled, he "was very conscious of being beaten in a way by circumstances and, for instance, government pressures."

This attitude arose from his experience as a public figure, which corroborated both his Manichaean vision and his fears. When moved by the latter, one executive remembered, "his hair would be all up in the air, and he'd have kind of a dark look in his eyes, and you wouldn't want to go near him at all." But often, in a short time, "he was a very congenial looking fellow."[13] With the passing years, Ford's moods oscillated increasingly between such extremes. During the 1930's Harry Bennett stimulated Ford's fears, as he slowly rose through the organization until nearly seizing control during the early 1940's. He played upon Ford, periodically reporting subversion within his plant, payroll robbery attempts, and threats to kidnap Edsel's children. Allegedly for protection, Bennett maintained ties with the underworld.

He eventually had a more powerful hold on Ford than even Edsel, and forced numerous old and trusted executives out of the company, including, finally, Sorensen, Henry's right-hand man for decades. As Nevins and Hill summarized:

Henry Ford's obsession with the idea that his beleaguering enemies were held back by Bennett's wall of defense was somehow sedulously nourished. One of Ford's remarks chills the blood. "The Jews and Communists," he said, "have been working on poor Harry until he's almost out of his mind." He needed a vacation. "Then he'll come back all ready to keep on fighting the ones who are trying to take over our plant." This harmonized with his statement to Fred L. Black: "The Ford Motor Company would be carried away, there wouldn't be anything left, if it wasn't for Harry."[14]

Bennett's increasing power was an index to Ford's growing fears. In the years immediately after World War I Ford had assumed that the "parasites" would be swept aside. The triumph of the Allies, the passage of prohibition, ever higher sales of the Model T, and national prosperity had all seemed to point toward the destruction of the old system and the beginning of a new era. Later, however, when Ford instead saw Europe rearming, prohibition repealed, car sales declining, unions on the rise, and the depression continuing, he relied upon Bennett to protect him from the forces which might "carry the company away," unless stoutly challenged.

And Ford's fears seemed to be extravagantly justified. He was attacked by Roosevelt's NRA, and his plant was the scene of the "Dearborn Massacre." However unjustified his use of violence to repel the weaponless marchers, his fears explain why Ford relied upon Bennett's kind of "protection." And when Ford discovered that the press supported the marchers, he became all the more convinced of the danger. Certainly his attitude toward unions did not soften in the later thirties, as the "Battle of the Overpass" indicates. Bennett became more powerful as the decade drew to a close, and Ford gradually developed the shrewd, suspicious, and somewhat cynical aspect Lochner first glimpsed. Increasingly, the benign, optimistic, even childlike figure whom Burroughs had known faded into the background.

However, that side of Ford did not disappear, but found expression in his work with Greenfield Village and other projects. He had already reconstructed his mother's home and several historic buildings, including the laboratory where Edison had invented his electric light. He carefully replicated all the important buildings of his own past and those of the nation's heritage he could procure. Simultaneously he continued to have the important scenes of his youth painted by Irving Bacon, whom he employed full time for that purpose, and renewed his interest in another old project, capturing earlier events in film recreations. His pivotal encounter with the road steam engine was filmed several times, but the most extraordinary film was that depicting his own childhood, with relations in the cast.[15]

After the Depression began, Ford sought out his mother's relatives and, to insure that all had jobs, brought five families to Dearborn, providing them with homes and clothing. Among these relatives, one woman looked much like his mother. The resemblance was strengthened, of course, by family ties, as her grandfather was Henry's cousin. But resemblance became identity when Ford met her daughter, Dorothy; Ford believed the young girl was his reincarnated mother, and until his death never wavered in this conviction. He wanted Dorothy to attend his Greenfield Village School, and when he discovered she was too old, he created a secondary school, allowing her to choose friends as classmates. She graduated with the first class and then attended the Edison Institute of Technology which Ford also created.[16]

During these years Ford spoke openly of his belief that the school-girl was his reincarnated mother, often referring to the matter in conversations with her parents. He also gave her an old china doll and a theosophical work, *Reincarnation, The Hope of the World.* Since she took little interest in the theory, Ford did not burden her with theological discussions, entertaining her with his knowledge of wildlife, taking her on a tour of the Rouge Steel Mill, and giving her driving lessons when she was sixteen. Dorothy still recalls that he used to duck down in his seat whenever they stopped at a traffic light, in order to escape the public's notice. Sometimes Ford called her home from his workshop, playing a tune on his Jew's harp by way of introduction and asking the family to guess the tune.

Ford also asked Irving Bacon to paint several scenes from childhood, with Dorothy as the model. As Bacon later recalled, "He said her resemblance to his mother was perfect."[17] After her marriage, which Henry and Clara attended, Ford asked the young couple if they would reenact his earliest years in a film, to be made at the restored Ford homestead, which still remained on its original site. Just as he had remembered the pattern of the parlor rug and the number of the kitchen stove, Ford now recalled the dresses his mother had worn and had two made for Dorothy to wear, while her husband was clad in the Sunday shirt and pants of the period.

The film opened with a view of zig-zagging split rail fence, and panned across a rough field dotted by stumps toward the Ford family walking across a field toward a log. They were reenacting Ford's first memory. Ford had written a description of the event in 1913:

The first thing that I remember in my life is my Father taking my brother John and myself to see a bird's nest under a large oak log twenty rods East of our Home and my birth place. John was so young that he could not walk   Father carried him I being two years older could run along with them this must have been about the year 1866 in June I remember the nest with 4 eggs and also the bird and hearing it sing I have always remembered the song and in later years found that it was a song sparrow. . . .[18]

Dorothy and her husband acted out this vignette. Through them Ford was attempting to recapture the first moments of his life, to re-discover its early rhythms and meanings. Earlier Ford had commissioned Irving Bacon to paint the same scene for the Henry Ford Museum, but evidently this static recreation was not enough, just as the static restoration of his mother's home had not been enough. With Ford, everything, including the past, had to come to life. If earlier he had declared that money must be based on a dynamic energy standard rather than on the static value of gold, if earlier he had transformed static production into the dynamic of the assembly line, now he found that the past itself must be subject to the same transformation. Rather than live in memory, his youth would live in the person of his reincarnated mother, and she would personally recreate the first scenes of his life. The film is an image of the American nuclear family living in idyllic simplicity and self-sufficiency on the frontier. The father figures only in the opening shots, and in the final six scenes the mother predominates, as she sorts and cleans vegetables, makes pancakes, sets the table, roasts corn on the fire, and spins.[19]

The focus and content of this film paralleled Ford's philosophy. The events of the first recollection would later find abstract expression in the belief in precognition, the emphasis on memory, and the quest for ex-perience. Whether Ford's recall was faithful to fact is less important than his arrangement and selection of events. His first memory was that of a discovery, to which he was guided by someone else. Because he could not understand the experience he retained it until later when he could comprehend it. Similarly, Ford's philosophy emphasized discovery, an-nounced that man required guidance by outside forces, and declared that a strong memory was essential in order to recall and assess experience.

Nor was the substitution of unseen forces in the philosophy for the father an accidental change. Reincarnation denied the father's importance; Ford became his own progenitor. The father was obliterated in the philosophy, while even in Ford's personal myth the emphasis fell on the discovery of the songbird and its nest, unhatched eggs, and incompre-hensible song. The conjunction of the emphasis on Ford's mother, his own conscious opening to the world, and the sparrow's eggs was a final touch which suggests that the memory was given a shape and coherence beyond the actual occurrence. He had returned to the beginning of his own personal time and had renewed his very inception through the agency of his reincarnated mother.

In his declining years he desperately needed such reproductions as his company slid further into debt; strikes, intrigues, and agitators beset his factories; and the lives of his grandchildren (so Bennett assured him) were constantly threatened. Caught in an apparently disintegrating world, Ford found two apparently incongruous extensions of his personality in Bennett and Dorothy. Through Bennett he defended his industrial empire and drove forward his projects; through Dorothy he retreated to the solace of childhood. These two sides to Ford did not belong to different periods of his life; nor did they reflect an inner struggle. They were extensions of the philosophical conclusions which had long been latent within him. After World War I they surfaced gradually in response to his experiences as a public figure. In a reaction curiously like Richard Nixon's, Ford's sentimental and even childlike side began to disappear as he retreated into greater isolation, relying more and more on his fears and vindictive executives.

Ford never relinquished his sentimental side, but rather turned it in other directions. In 1901 reincarnation had provided an explanation of events, when, nearing middle age, Ford had found himself with uncertain prospects. Now, in the closing years of his life he sought another vindication. In adolescence, after Mary Ford's death, the family house had seemed "like a watch without its mainspring." In middle age reincarnation had provided a new driving mechanism. And now, near death, when the world seemed to be disintegrating, Ford rediscovered his mother and recreated his origins. Her reappearance was tangible proof of his philosophy, physical evidence of reincarnation.

Ford's psychology thus was intimately intertwined with both his personal philosophy and his own myth of origins. His philosophy not only sanctioned spontaneity and intuition, but implied a relationship to his parents. Reincarnation denied the potency of his father; precognition rested upon an intuitive relationship with his mother. And since reincarnation abolished death, the core of personality—Ford's and his mother's—would never disappear.

An earlier chapter closed with a description of Ford's central struggle for a balance between body and mind, farm and factory, production and consumption. His actions emphasized the concrete, as he sought pragmatic solutions to problems. The hallmark of his imagination was this ability to get at the root of a problem while maintaining at the same time a larger view of its relations to other problems. Thus, if farmers would not sell their crops, industry must find uses for them, or both would fail. If men were unhealthy, then they must find new foods and adopt more abstemious diets. If the economy faltered or workers went on strike, then parasites, bankers, or a conspiracy must be the cause, and a new basis for monetary value was the solution. No money? Banks at fault. No work? Man at fault, probably lazy. Prisons fail? Because they are unproductive. Ford's mind found few abstract solutions to the problems of modern life, but focused intently on the point of failure, sometimes mistook a symptom for a cause, and confidently ignored warnings of failure.

A man of unusual self-assurance, he relied upon his intuitions, as his "mind jumped from one subject to another very strikingly." Never at a loss for words, he spoke in a fluent and simple vocabulary, typically "in very short, telegraphic type sentences." His mind was quick, and he seldom needed to be taught, or told, a thing twice. He exerted a kind of magnetism, which may be partially explained by his assurance, simplicity, and intelligence, but which resists complete explanation. As the years passed his moods became more pronounced, and the shrewd, suspicious businessman came to dominate the idealistic and boyish humanitarian, until, in his last years, he relied on a private police force for protection against the forces his Manichaean mind knew to be there.

And yet, when free of these fears, his was a mind admirably suited to solving the technical problems encountered in building an automobile. Like Edison, Ford was tireless, made no *a priori* assumptions about what might work, and would try every conceivable possibility. Ford was especially prone to believe that simplicity in design was a virtue, and that heavy, complex, or unwieldy machines were a sign of failure. So the Model T was lightweight, simple enough for any farmer to repair, and easy to maneuver.

More than one commentator felt that the car represented Ford's mind in mechanical form, perhaps none expressing this so well as Samuel Marquis. In his words, "The Ford car is Henry Ford done in steel and other things . . . power and endurance in engine and chassis, but somewhat ephemeral in its upper works."[20] Dynamic, functional, without ornament, the Model T mirrored the lean strapping man and his abrupt manner, sudden moods, uncanny intuition, hard work, and simple ideas; like him, it possessed a universal appeal. His "upper works," apparently but afterthoughts, were largely forgotten.

# PART 3

# PRESERVING NATURE'S ORDER

*"When its errands are noble and adequate, a steamboat bridging the Atlantic between Old and New England and arriving at its ports with the punctuality of a planet, is a step of man into harmony with nature. . . ."*

Emerson, "Art"

*"The Machine is the new messiah."*

Henry Ford

# CHAPTER EIGHT

# THE MACHINE IS THE
# NEW MESSIAH

While few were interested in Ford's mind, Americans attributed more to him than he deserved. He appeared to many as the sole architect of a second industrial revolution, when in fact both the assembly line and the Model T were largely created by the engineers who worked under Ford's direction. Ford overshadowed them in the public mind. He seemed to possess immense creative power because the average American demanded such a figure in compensation for his own insignificance, and because he seemed to demonstrate the equation of individual success and national progress. Furthermore, because Americans tended to confuse natural fact and social construction, Ford's natural mien and rural background were appropriate ingredients in the creation of a symbolic figure who could mediate between the world of machines and the pastoral world.

Ford himself conceived of machines as natural facts, and he attempted to shape a new world through the elimination of all inessential parts, whether in automobiles or in the banking community. In attempting to fuse the machine and the garden, Emerson had also succumbed to the "technological sublime" in the decade before 1844, believing that "machinery and transcendentalism agree well," that mechanization would thrust Americans into closer contact with their continent, and that consequently the writer's duty was to perceive the new machines as "new and necessary facts" in essential harmony with nature. The belief that industrialization could be purified and made a natural force united with spiritual forces also underlay the American vernacular tradition in art and architecture, a tradition which demanded that efficiency and function determine form. This aesthetics, promulgated by Horatio Greenough, Emerson, Louis Sullivan, and Frank Lloyd Wright, self-consciously condemned the creation of beauty for its own sake, arguing instead that true beauty emerged in the functional lines of natural objects. As Emerson wrote in a passage which Ford would later underline, the "division of beauty from use the laws of nature do not permit. As soon as beauty is sought, not from religion or love, but for pleasure, it degrades the seeker."

The vernacular tradition which expressed this philosophy found expression in such creations as the clipper ship, the American ax, the loosely jointed American steam engine, the new architecture of Sullivan and Wright, and of course, in the Model T car. Emerson wished to transform the work of the businessman, and later Ford proved an apt disciple. Like the architect, the inventor must abjure all tradition and "study with hope and love the precise thing to be done by him, considering the climate, the soil, the length of the day, the wants of the people, the habit and form of government."[1] Ford had found the precise task—to build a reliable and inexpensive automobile which every man in a seminomadic America could own and drive. He had considered the need for a car which would run in any weather, a car maneuverable and set high off the winding, rutted roads. He had considered the length of the working man's day, and finding it too long, had constructed a car that would shift work formerly done by muscle and bone to iron and steel. The Model T could saw wood, plow fields, draw water, and haul produce. And in accord with the American ideal of equality, all Fords were the same. It thus embodied an egalitarian social philosophy and merged with the landscape while simultaneously helping transform the agrarian democracy it seemed to represent. Such inventions appeared natural; in operation they were profoundly social.

The same confusion of the artificial with the natural characterized the public enthusiasm for the Muscle Shoals project, the interest in the Model A, the nostalgia for the Model T, and the reluctance to give up Ford as a symbolic figure during the 1930's. But it was not merely the automobile or the assembly line in particular which could be misconstrued; Americans tended to perceive all mechanization as a natural force beyond control and assumed that the creation and proliferation of machines such as the automobile were inevitable and in some mystical way essential to progress.

In fact, many were ready to reinterpret America's past to make industrialization the central factor which made the New World separate from the Old. American "know-how" and "ingenuity" became hallmarks of a consciousness not simply transformed by contact with the wilderness, but manifested in the machines which transformed the wilderness. In this new myth, utopia ceased to be a purely agrarian ideal, and the inventor achieved new prominence as the representative American. The frontiersman was but his harbinger. Eli Whitney, George Washington Carver, Alexander Graham Bell, Thomas Edison, and Henry Ford became prototypes of the Promethean hero who wrested secrets from Nature and used them to hasten the transformation of an imperfect society.

The change from the frontier hero to the inventive hero preserved the belief in a naturally functioning economy. Most Americans never articulated Henry Ford's belief that an invisible consciousness guided their national welfare, but nevertheless acted as though such a force guided their affairs. A beneficent Providence oversaw the Manifest Destiny of the nineteenth century; an industrial economy functioned according to natural law. Neither view made a distinction between nature and civilization, and both visualized a future of unlimited freedom and material welfare.

This future could only be approached in fantasy through a special sense of time combined with a belief in the uniqueness of American civilization. To the nineteenth-century American, time seemed linear, life was a series of unrepeatable acts, personality was formed by an irrevocable accretion of events, and existence appeared as a passage. Because of this irreversible flow of events, eschatology was personal, not social, and took the form of a recurring dream of pastoral retreat and renewal through an escape from time. The characteristic heroes were the frontiersmen.

But to the twentieth-century American, time assumed a new quality as the assembly line became a new organizing principle. Time became more segmented. While linear, it also became capable of replication in events such as the film or the recording. Leisure no longer implied rest, but took on the character of a marathon or an endurance test. Americans had often been accused of an inability to relax, but now, rather than being preoccupied with his business, the American, whose business was routinized, increasingly achieved identity by assembling experiences. The automobile allowed one to move quickly from place to place, enhancing the illusion of freedom and increasing the number of acts, the duplication of experiences. The construction of self became nearly identical with the consumption and replication of experience; industrialism seemed to promise release from the irrevocability which events had stamped upon character in earlier centuries.

The characteristic hero of this industrial culture, both symbolically and personally, was Henry Ford. His peculiar theory of reincarnation opened the possibility of recreating not only himself, but all society. The industrial Adam would make all things new again; he would even replace the animals with immaculate machines. Ford discovered the liberation of a "long view of life" which did not impose a consciousness attained through historical events, absolved him from responsibility for his actions, and allowed experience to be replicated, mass produced, and replayed. Actions were no longer chained together in an endless skein. He overcame time itself through the replication of earlier events and by speeding up future events through the assembly line. He had time to create, to duplicate infinitely. The car would reappear in a series of lifetimes; "Three worlds from now the Ford will be a better car than ever before, because of the experience gained." He could improve the next life by focusing on the material facts of this world. The Model T was an engine of salvation.

The replication and acceleration of events unleashed continuous action. Ford's personality seemed malleable, his existence unlimited, but American society might disintegrate and could only be saved by technology if its enemies were driven from power. Ford believed that previous civilizations far more advanced than his had been destroyed countless times before, and that "once upon a time the human race actually knew the things which they now say they believe or hold by faith." He believed "that something has happened to the race; it has fallen under a cloud, and things that once were clear as day and of common knowledge, are now so misty that we must hold them by faith." The myth of a lost Eden or golden era coupled with the belief that "the race has fallen under a cloud" are the characteristic expressions of archaic, as well as modern man's, awareness of spiritual impoverishment. But where through ritual primitive man periodically recovers that lost golden era, destroying chaos, modern man has increasingly relied upon his manipulation and control of the environment to strive toward a golden era in the future, while excoriating those who reject that dream or seem to stand in its way. Thus the belief in technological progress and the search for scapegoats when that progress is not achieved are linked as manifestations of modern man's search for renewal.

The result of confusing Nature and Civilization was twofold: the industrialist leader became messianic; those who opposed him became unnatural. The pattern of Ford's images reveals why Americans demanded not only the transformation of the physical world but also the recreation of others in their own image. The existence of cultural or ideological differences reopened the rift between Nature and Civilization, and by logical extension ultimately threatened the belief that "natural laws" governed society. The immigrant, the black, the Jew, the Marxist, had to be assimilated or expelled—for toleration required a recognition of the artificiality of culture and human institutions.

Over the years Ford had repeatedly tried to homogenize his work force, to make his employees identical in language, custom, and self-reliance. His village industries were to be run by natural, whole men who had shaken off all vestiges of foreign custom, reborn in the melting pot of his factory. As his productive capacity grew, his fears of agitators increased. As the assembly line raced toward a nearly instantaneous creation, Ford expected its mechanical perfection to force men forward. By speeding up events, the assembly line and the Model T would overcome time. Ford knew that "Time waste differs from material waste in that there can be no salvage." He knew the difference between time and all else that made up his world. Unlike the raw materials that were his earth, the human body which could be repaired through proper diet, or the conspiracies that could be exposed and defeated, time alone could not be shaped to Ford's will. There was no last judgment, but there was the test of time, and only machinery could save the imperfect world. Redemption could not spring from nature or the human heart unaided. Ford had discovered, "The Machine is the new messiah."[2]

This study has moved from the outermost shell of cultural values expressed in Ford's public images through the structure of his ideas toward a confrontation with the medium of consciousness itself, or time. The linear nature of western time and the search for a secular salvation informs the interplay between public and private values and gives them a common direction. The Protestant tradition of redemption through work achieved a new expression in the assembly line, as ascetic discipline became routinized in a factory environment. In the context of a dying Christian fundamentalism and during the transformation of America from an agricultural to an industrial nation, Ford symbolized the process of secularization and emerged as a new kind of American hero.

While the quasi-religious nature of his public role remained hidden and his personal religious code unknown, Ford gave direction and meaning to American life. In an extension of the archaic smith's role, he forged the raw materials of the world into more perfect forms and signified the potential for human perfection. His transformation of the environment, like the vernacular tradition in American design, had an eschatological significance, changing the terms of one's being-in-the-world.

In early society, the intrusion of a new form of matter into the cosmos always had a religious meaning. Those who manipulated the living ores dug from the womb of the earth interfered with natural processes, and consequently, the smith figure was clothed in power and bore affinities with both the shaman and the warrior, just as Ford inherited the attributes of the messiah and the frontiersman. The smith was a master of fire, and he could transform the material world in a way analogous to the shaman's manipulation of spiritual powers. Like the warrior, whose weapons he provided, the smith recapitulated the acts of the gods. His hammering was thunder, his forge the womb of creation, and his products were often thought to be alive. Because of these powers the smith was revered and feared by his society. Similarly, Ford seemed to make animate objects, such as the bombers "coughing with life," the Tin Lizzie, or the airplane dubbed the "Tin Goose." And like the smith, Ford experienced the ambivalence of his culture because he tampered with the structure of the world.

In a national ideology that both identified the conquest of nature as progress and idealized a pastoral retreat from civilization, Ford functioned as the mediating figure. His machines partook of both worlds; they were mechanical, yet had life and personality. Similarly, Ford was both farmer and mechanic. Ford's products and his apparent character denied that a continuing assault on the environment had destroyed harmony with nature. Both publically and in his personal philosophy, Ford helped perpetuate the illusory synthesis of technology and the pastoral world, the illusion which drove the dominant American mind through time.

Archaic man had sought the absolution from previous experience
in the repetition of cosmological myths in ritual, thereby beginning
the world over again. The Christian found absolution in a symbolic reenactment of the Crucifixion, renewing and cleansing himself. But
the industrial American could not be absolved by the repetitious labor
of the assembly line. He could only imitate the replication of experience
it suggested and seek the perfection of form it promised. The acceleration of events, the blurred images of life that rushed past, the
numb mania for consumption, offered no release from previous error.
Ford was released by his belief in an unseen guiding force and his cer-
tainty that in another life he would perfect both himself and his world.
But his contemporaries were caught in a "furious steeplechase toward
nothing," seeking an orgiastic future that year by year receded.[3] Victims
of an illusory mechanical victory, in seeking regeneration they completed the rape of the land the frontiersman had begun.

# NOTES

### INTRODUCTION

1.    For example, John William Ward and Henry Nash Smith, whose works pre-date Levi-Strauss and are not as functionalist as their definition would imply. For a thorough discussion, see Cecil F. Tate's *The Search for a Method in American Studies* (Minneapolis, University of Minnesota Press, 1973).

2.    Theodore P. Greene, *America's Heroes* (New York: Oxford University Press, 1970), p. 7. John William Ward, *Andrew Jackson: Symbol for an Age* (New York: Oxford Press, 1955), p. 213.

3.    Claude Levi-Strauss, *The Raw and the Cooked* (New York: Harper & Row, 1969); Mircea Eliade, *Myths, Dreams and Mysteries* (New York: Harper & Row, 1960). For comment on their differences, see G. S. Kirk, *Myth* (Berkeley: University of California Press, 1973).

### 1. AN IGNORANT IDEALIST

1.    On character, see John Cawelti, *Apostles of the Self-Made Man* (Chicago: University of Chicago Press, 1965). On mobility, see Stephen Thernstrom, *Poverty and Progress* (New York: Atheneum, 1973).

2.    Sidney Olson, *Young Henry Ford* (Detroit: Wayne State University Press, 1963), p. 90. Much of what follows is treated in more detail in Allan Nevins, *Ford: The Times, the Man, the Company* (New York: Charles Scribner's Sons, 1954).

3.    Olson, *Young Henry Ford,* pp. 176–77.

4.    Ford Archives, Newspaper Files. A summary of press reactions may be found in *Literary Digest,* January 17, 1914, p. 95.

5.    Horace L. Arnold and Fay Leon Faurote, *Ford Methods and Ford Shops* (Detroit: Industrial Management, 1915).

6.    *Detroit Free Press,* August 22, 1915.

7.    Ford Archives, Newspaper Files; *Literary Digest,* December 11, 1915, pp. 1333–36.

8.    See Reynold M. Wik, *Henry Ford and Grass Roots America* (Ann Arbor, Michigan: University of Michigan Press, 1972).

9.    Greene, *America's Heroes,* final chapter.

10.    On the trial: Ford Archives, Newspaper Files; Keith Sward, *The Legend of Henry Ford* (New York: Rinehart & Company, 1948), pp. 103–5; *Nation,* July 26, 1919, p. 102; *Literary Digest,* August 9, 1919, pp. 44–46; *Chicago Herald,* July 16, 1919; Wik, *Henry Ford,* p. 54.

11.    There are many Ford jokebooks in the Ford Archives. Also see David L. Lewis, "A Survey of Ford Jokes," *The Horseless Carriage Gazette,* January-February, 1973, pp. 22–26.

12.    Gordon W. Davidson, *Henry Ford: The Formation and Course of a Public Figure* (unpublished dissertation, Columbia University, 1966), p. 266.

13.    Wik, *Henry Ford,* p. 216; *American Magazine,* February, 1919, pp. 33–37.

## 2. COME AND LEAD US OUT

1.    See Roderick Nash, *The Nervous Generation* (Chicago: Rand McNally, 1970) and Clarke A. Cambers, *Seedtime of Reform* (Minneapolis: University of Minnesota Press, 1963).

2.    Harold Stearns, *Civilization in the United States* (New York: Harcourt Brace, 1922).

3.    Robert T. Handy, *A Christian America,* (New York: Oxford University Press, 1974), pp. 186–207. *Literary Digest,* May 15, 1915, pp. 1155–56.

4.    *Denver Post,* September 22, 1920.

5.    Robert S. Lynd and Helen Merrell Lynd, *Middletown* (New York: Harcourt Brace, 1929).

6.    Ford Archives, Accession no. 163.

7.    Ford Archives, Newspaper Files; *Literary Digest,* January 28, 1922, p. 10; *Illustrated World,* April, 1922, p. 184.

8.    *Nation,* December 20, 1922, and January 24, 1923; and Sward, *Legend of Henry Ford,* pp. 127–31.

9.    *Collier's Weekly Magazine,* July 14, 1923, p. 5; *Literary Digest,* June 30, 1923; *Forum,* July, 1924, p. 34; sample cartoons collected in *Literary Digest,* February 10, 1923; *New Republic,* July 25, 1923, p. 222; *Current Opinion,* July, 1923, pp. 9–11.

10.    *Literary Digest,* February 10, 1923, and October 27, 1923.

11.    Quoted in Wik, *Henry Ford,* p. 175.

12.    Davidson, *Henry Ford,* p. 163. Ford war profits were $926,780.

13.    *Forum,* July, 1924; reprinted, *Literary Digest,* July 12, 1924.

14.    William Stidger, *Henry Ford: The Man and His Motives* (New York: George H. Doran, 1923), pp. 113–18.

15.    Wik, *Henry Ford,* p. 54; (hymn) Ford Archives, Accession no. 42, Box 2.

16.    B. A. Botkin, "The Lore of the Lizzie Label," *American Speech,* December, 1930, p. 85.

17.    Edwin Wildman, *Famous Leaders of Industry* (Boston: The Page Company, 1920), pp. 131–47; Archibald Henderson, *Contemporary Immortals* (New York: Appleton and Company, 1930), pp. 177–93; Allen Frederick, *The Story of Famous Fortunes* (Chicago: 1929); and Niven Busch, *Twenty-One Americans* (New York: Doubleday, Doran & Co., 1930), pp. 3–48. Quote from Busch, p. 35.

18.    *Nation,* "The King Is Dead" and "Strut Miss Lizzie," December 14, 1927.

19.    Quoted in Mircea Eliade's *Myth and Reality* (New York: Harper & Row, 1968), p. 187.

20.    *New York American,* December 1, 1927, p. 1; *Detroit News,* December 1, 1927, p. 1; *New Orleans States,* December 2, 1927, p. 1; *Newark News,* December 1, 1927, p. 1; "Greatest Show on Earth," *Independent,* December 31, 1927, p. 650.

21.    Henry Adams, *The Education of Henry Adams* (Boston: Houghton Mifflin, 1961), p. 380.

### 3. BREAD AND BULLETS

1.    Henry Ford, *My Life and Work* (New York: Doubleday, Page, 1922), and *Moving Forward* (New York: Doubleday, 1930); *Nation,* December 17, 1930, p. 681; *New York Times,* October 26, 1930, p. 1; *Survey,* November 15, 1930, p. 229.

2.    *Nation,* February 17, 1932, p. 204; *New Republic,* February 10, 1932, p. 354; *New Statesman,* February 6, 1932, p. 172; *Forum,* May, 1932; *Outlook,* March, 1932, p. 192; *Saturday Review,* February 6, 1932, p. 152.

3.    Jonathan Norton Leonard, *The Tragedy of Henry Ford* (New York: G. P. Putnam's Sons, 1932), pp. 11, 13, 241–45.

4.    Paul Oliver, *Blues Fell This Morning* (London: Cassell Press, 1960), pp. 30–32.

5.    Walter Cunningham, *J 8* (North American Publishing Co., ca. 1930), p. 9.

6.    Edmund Wilson, "Detroit Motors," *New Republic,* March 25, 1931; Richard Pells, *Radical Visions and American Dreams* (New York: Harper & Row, 1973), p. 161.

7.    *Los Angeles Illustrated Daily News,* March 9, 1932; *Colorado Springs Gazette,* March 9, 1932; *Philadelphia Evening Public Ledger,* March 9, 1932; *Pittsburgh Post Gazette,* March 9, 1932.

8.    "Henry Ford Swims the Red Sea" (Indianapolis: The Fellowship Press, ca. 1941).

9.    *Detroit News; Detroit Free Press; Detroit Times; Buffalo Evening Gazette;* all March 9, 1932. *Nation,* March 3, 1932.

10.    On the NRA see Sidney Fine, *The Automobile under the Blue Eagle* (Ann Arbor: University of Michigan Press, 1963); *Nation,* November 8, 1933; *New Republic,* September 13, 1933.

11.    Robert L. Cruden, *The End of the Ford Myth* (New York: International Pamphlets, 1932), pp. 3, 13–15.

12.    E. B. White, "Farewell My Lovely," reprinted in Mary Moline (ed.) *The Best of Ford* (Van Nuys, California: Rumbleseat Press, 1973), pp. 240, 246, 252.

13.    Leo Marx, *The Machine in the Garden* (New York: Oxford Press, 1964), pp. 5–11.

14.    Ibid., pp. 7–8.

15.    Wayne State Labor Archives, Accession no. 125, Box 1.

16.    William E. Leuchtenburg, *Franklin D. Roosevelt and the New Deal* (New York: Harper & Row, 1963), pp. 244, 264.

17.    Allan Nevins and Frank Hill, *Ford: Decline and Rebirth* (New York: Charles Scribner's Sons, 1962), pp. 140–41.

18.    *United Auto Worker,* May 13, 1939; Upton Sinclair, *The Flivver King* (Detroit: United Auto Workers of America, 1937), p. 113; Carl Raushenbush, *Fordism* (League for Industrial Democracy, 1937), p. 7.

19.    Wayne State Labor Archives, verticle file, under Ford.

20.    Wayne State Labor Archives, People's Song Library, Box 10, folder 1.

21.    Cover story, *Time,* March 23, 1942; pp. 10–14.

22.    Sigmund Diamond, *The Reputation of American Businessmen* (Cambridge: Harvard University Press, 1955), p. 175.

23.    Alfred Jones, *Roosevelt's Image Brokers* (Port Washington, New York: Kennikat Press, 1974).

## 4. I BELONG WITH THE BUDDHIST CROWD

1. "I Belong with the Buddhist Crowd," statement made to Allan Benson, *The New Henry Ford* (New York: Funk & Wagnalls, 1923), p. 326; *Rotarian*, January 1947, 9; *Detroit Times*, August 26, 1928; Orlando Smith, *Eternalism: A Theory of Infinite Justice* (Boston: Houghton Mifflin, 1902); Ralph Waldo Trine and Henry Ford, *The Power That Wins* (Indianapolis: Bobbs-Merrill, 1928), p. 146.

2. Trine and Ford, *Power That Wins*, pp. 14, 80; *Forum*, April, 1928, p. 484.

3. *American Magazine*, April, 1921; *Literary Digest*, January 7, 1928; Ralph Waldo Emerson, "Self-Reliance," first paragraph.

4. *Forum*, August, 1919; see notebooks in the Ford Archives, Accession no. 1, Box 17.

5. *Literary Digest*, January 7, 1928; *Forbes Magazine*, January 21, 1928, p. 10; *Forum*, March, 1928, p. 364.

6. Trine and Ford, *Power That Wins*, pp. 145, 181.

7. Samuel Marquis, *Henry Ford, An Interpretation* (Chicago, 1922), p. 50.

8. *New Republic*, October 31, 1923; *Scribner's Magazine*, July, 1931, p. 30; Allan Nevins and Frank Hill, *Ford: Expansion and Challenge* (New York: Charles Scribner's Sons, 1957), pp. 614–16; Edsel's remark comes from the reminiscences of the Oral History Project directed by Henry E. Edmunds, director of the Ford Archives, and supervised by Owen Bombard. Over three hundred interviews were conducted with relatives, friends, domestics, business associates, and social acquaintances. Some, as in this case, have restricted use of their names.

9. Rosamund Harding, *The Anatomy of Inspiration* (Cambridge, England: W. Heffer, 1948). See also Arthur Koestler's *The Act of Creation* (New York: Dell Publishing Co., 1967), p. 145.

10. *Rotarian*, January, 1947, 9–11; Trine and Ford, *Power That Wins*, p. 170.

11. *New York Times*, October 29, 1921; and interview with Bruce Barton, *American Magazine*, April, 1921, pp. 7–9.

12. *Rotarian*, January, 1947; *American Magazine*, April, 1921; Trine and Ford, *Power That Wins*, p. 107.

13. *New York American*, April 30, 1925; Benson, *New Henry Ford*, p. 264.

14. Trine and Ford, *Power That Wins*, p. 108; *New York Times*, May 20, 1922; Ford Archives, Accession no. 1, Box 15.

15. "Reminiscences of J. L. McCloud," Ford Archives; *New York Times*, May 11, 1926, and March 5, 1930; *Redbook*, June, 1930.

16. Ford Archives, Accession no. 1, Box 17; *Rotarian*, January 1947, p. 10.

17. *Literary Digest*, September 30, 1922.

18. Olson, *Young Henry Ford*, p. 29.

19. Harvey S. Firestone, "My Vacations with Ford and Edison," *System*, May and July, 1926; Ford Archives, Accession no. 1, Box 14.

20. *American Magazine*, April, 1921, p. 9; John Reed, interview, *Metropolitan Magazine*, October, 1916.

21. Sward, *Legend of Henry Ford*, p. 112.

22. Trine and Ford, *Power That Wins*, p. 145; *Forum*, April, 1928.

23. *Forum*, November, 1928; Ford Archives, Accession no. 1, Box 14.

24. "Put the Bible Back in School," *Good Housekeeping*, April, 1924.

## 5. TO STOP WARS BY DESTROYING COWS

1.   Henry Ford, *365 of Henry Ford's Sayings* (New York: The League for a Living, 1923) number 282; Gabriel Kolko, *The Triumph of Conservatism* (Chicago: Quadrangle Books, 1963), pp. 11–30.

2.   Nevins and Hill, *Ford: Expansion and Challenge,* pp. 673–83; *Forum,* April, 1928, p. 483.

3.   *Literary Digest,* August 19, 1922; *System,* May, 1924, pp. 665–66.

4.   E. G. Pipp, *The Real Henry Ford* (Detroit: Pipp's Weekly, 1922), p. 14. Samuel Marquis, *Henry Ford, An Interpretation* (Boston: Little Brown, 1923), pp. 20–23.

5.   Ford Archives, Accession no. 1, Box 14; *New York Times,* August 18, 1928.

6.   *Illustrated World,* May, 1922, p. 347.

7.   *Scientific American,* July, 1926, p. 40.

8.   *Forbes Magazine,* January 21, 1928, p. 11; *System,* May, 1924, p. 611.

9.   Marquis, *Henry Ford,* p. 155.

10.   *System,* January, 1926, pp. 38–39; *Metropolitan Magazine,* October, 1926, p. 67.

11.   Ralph Waldo Emerson, *Selected Writings* (New York: Modern Library, 1950), p. 46.

12.   *Forbes Magazine,* January 21, 1928, p. 11.

13.   *System,* January 1926, p. 38; *American Magazine,* April, 1921, p. 9; *Literary Digest,* February, 1926, p. 42.

14.   Ford Archives, Accession no. 1, Box 15; *New York Times,* September 9, 1923, section 5; *Literary Digest,* February, 1926, p. 42; *Detroit News,* July 16, 1936.

15.   *Rotarian,* February, 1943, pp, 15–18.

16.   *Outlook,* July 28, 1926, p. 439; *New York Times,* October 26, 1921, p. 1.

17.   *Rotarian,* September, 1933, p. 59; Christy Borth, *Pioneers of Plenty* (New York: Bobbs-Merrill, 1933), pp. 17, 22.

18.   Ford Archives, Reminiscences of J. L. McCloud, Oral History Series, 15–17. *American Magazine,* April, 1921, p. 122.

19.   *System,* May and July, 1926, p. 793; *System,* May, 1924, p. 662.

20.   *Illustrated World,* May, 1922, p. 348; *Outlook,* October, 1923, p. 300.

21.   *New York Times,* December 4, 1921, p. 1; *Forum,* November, 1928, p. 683.

22.   *New York Times,* December 4, 1921, pp, 1, 20; *Detroit News,* June 1, 1922, p. 7; *Illustrated World,* April, 1922, p. 184.

23.   *Forum,* April, 1928, p. 487; *New York Times,* December 2, 1921, p. 1.

24.   *Atlantic,* March, 1931, pp. 288–95; *Rotarian,* February, 1943, p. 58; *Collier's Magazine,* March 22, 1924.

25.   *Illustrated World,* May, 1922, p. 342; Ford Archives, Accession no. 1, Boxes 13 and 14; *New York Times,* May 11, 1926, p. 6.

26.   *New York Times,* February 5, 1927; see also, "Aren't We All Killers?" *Collier's Magazine,* June 11, 1927.

27.   Ford Archives, Accession no. 1, Box 13; *Ford Ideals,* from the *Dearborn Independent* (Dearborn, Michigan: Dearborn Publishing Co., 1922), p. 308.

28.   Gustavus Meyers, *History of Bigotry in the United States* (New York: Random House, 1943), chapters 16, 17, and 28; H. R. Trevor-Roper, *The European Witch Craze of the Sixteenth and Seventeenth Centuries* (New York: Harper & Row, 1969), p. 122.

29.   Richard Hofstadter, *The Age of Reform* (New York: Random House, 1955), 81; Ford Archives, Oral History Series, name withheld by request; *Detroit Free Press,* December 1, 1938, p. 1.

## 6. BY INSTINCT AN ENGINEER

1.    Ford Archives, Accession no. 1, Box 13; Ralph Waldo Emerson, *Selected Writings* (New York: Random House, 1950), 194; Ford Archives, Accession no. 1, Box 1.

2.    Anne Jardim, *The First Henry Ford* (Cambridge: M.I.T. Press, 1970). Margaret Ford Ruddiman, "Memories of My Brother Henry Ford," *Michigan History,* Vol. 37, no. 3, p. 248; Ford Archives, Anne Hood Manuscript, 24. Jardim's excessive reliance on Mrs. Ruddiman mars her interesting approach. When Mrs. Ruddiman was interviewed she was extremely old and had to be prompted continually by the interviewers as she attempted to recall events which occurred before she had reached the age of ten. Jardim seldom mentions Ford's mother, never discusses Ford's belief in reincarnation, and argues that he was stagnant in later life.

3.    Ruddiman, "Memories," pp. 248, 251, 247, 238.

4.    Nevins and Hill, *Ford: The Times,* p. 641; Ruddiman, "Memories," p. 238; *American Magazine,* July, 1923, pp. 13–14.

5.    Allan Benson, *The New Henry Ford* (New York: Funk & Wagnalls, 1923), 111. Interview, "I believe in a Master Mind" *London Express,* November 4, 1928.

6.    Ford Archives, Anne Hood Manuscript, pp. 36–38; Ford Archives, Accession no. 1, Box 13; *American Magazine,* July, 1923, p. 14.

7.    Olson, *Young Henry Ford,* p. 20; Ford Archives, Anne Hood Manuscript, p. 36; Ford Archives, Accession no. 1, Box 1; Ruddiman, "Memories," p. 238.

8.    Olson, *Young Henry Ford,* pp. 27–59; Nevins and Hill, *Ford: The Times,* p. 83.

9.    Ford Archives, Anne Hood Manuscript, pp. 63–65; Charles B. King, *Psychic Reminiscences* (private edition, 1935), p. 5; Ford Archives, Accession no. 1, Box 1.

10.    Henry Ford, *Edison as I Knew Him* (New York: Cosmopolitan Book Co., 1930), pp. 3–5, 7, 12, 14.

11.    Olson, *Young Henry Ford,* p. 58; Nevins and Hill, *Ford: The Times,* pp. 191–93.

12.    Ford Archives, Reminiscences of Oliver E. Barthel, p. 70; see also interview with Henry Ford in *Detroit Times,* April 26, 1938; Orlando Smith, "A Short View of Great Questions" was later incorporated into the same author's *Eternalism: A Theory of Infinite Justice* (Boston: Houghton Mifflin and Co., 1902). A copy of the pamphlet was found in Ford's personal papers after his death. *London Express,* November 4, 1928.

13.    Ford, *Edison as I Knew Him,* p. 12; *London Express,* November 4, 1928.

14.    *American Magazine,* July, 1923, p. 13; Ford Archives, Reminiscences of Oliver E. Barthel, pp. 71, 73; Benson, *New Henry Ford,* p. 332.

15.    See Richard Chase for a summary in *Walt Whitman Reconsidered* (New York: William Sloan Associates, 1955), pp. 33–57; on Melville see F. O. Matthiessen, *American Renaissance* (New York: Oxford University Press, 1968), p. 373.

16.    *London Express,* November 4, 1928.

## 7. THE WATCH'S MAINSPRING

1.    Ford Archives, Clara Ford Papers, Accession no. 1, Box 22; John Burroughs, *John Burroughs Talks* (Boston: Houghton Mifflin, 1922), p. 326.

2.    Ford Archives, Reminiscences of C. J. Smith, p. 52; *New Orleans States,* December 11, 1927; Ford Archives, Reminiscences of J. L. McCloud, p. 354; Reminiscences of Harold M. Cordell, p. 93; Frank Hill Papers, Accession no. 940, Box 7.

3.  *New York Herald,* January 1, 1915, p. 1. On Edison, see *The Diary and Sundry Observations of Thomas Alva Edison* (New York: Philosophical Library, 1948), pp. 203-44.
4.  *Pipp's Weekly,* May 15, 1920, p. 7. Fords' copy of Emerson, Ford Archives, Accession no. 1, Box 15.
5.  Sward, *Legend of Henry Ford,* pp. 101-5, 120-23, 151-57; Marquis, *Henry Ford,* p. 9.
6.  Louis P. Lochner, *America's Don Quixote* (London: Kegan Paul, Trench, Truber & Co., Ltd., 1924), p. 1; Benson, *New Henry Ford,* p. 325; Marquis, *Henry Ford,* p. 169.
7.  Burroughs, *Burroughs Talks,* p. 326; Benson, *New Henry Ford,*pp. 356-57; Ford Archives, Reminiscences, name withheld.
8.  *New Republic,* November 14, 1928; Ford Archives, Reminiscences of J. L. McCloud, p. 391; cartoon in *Des Moines Register,* September 30, 1927.
9.  W. Atkinson, *Reincarnation and the Law of Karma* (Yogi Publishing Society, date and place not given); Ann Besant, *Reincarnation: Its Necessity* (Manas Press, no place, no date); copies of the other books not obtainable, Frank Campsall, Ford's assistant secretary ordered them in 1922; see Ford Archives, Accession no. 572, Box 10. Trine and Ford, *Power That Wins,* pp. 11, 12, 15, 20-21.
10.  Ford Archives, articles by C. J. Armstrong available in Ford's scrapbooks.
11.  *Detroit News,* February 2, 1926.
12.  William C. Richards, *The Last Billionaire* (New York: Charles Scribner's Sons, 1948), pp. 149-50; Marquis, *Henry Ford,* pp. 78, 89.
13.  Ford Archives, Reminiscences of the Reverend Hedley Stacey, p. 32; Frank Hill Papers, Accession no. 940, Box 7.
14.  Allan Nevins and Frank Hill, *Ford: Decline and Rebirth* (New York: Charles Scribner's Sons, 1954), p. 262.
15.  National Archives, Ford Film Collection, 200 FC-4014, 200 FC-3853, 200 FC-2074(b).
16.  This information and subsequent material largely based upon two interviews with Mrs. Dorothy Heber, who was introduced to me by the staff of the Ford Archives.
17.  Ford Archives, Reminiscences of Irving Bacon, pp. 123, 149.
18.  Henry Ford Museum, notebook in sealed glass case, with passage quoted visible. Reproduced in Olson, *Young Henry Ford,* p. 14.
19.  National Archives, Ford Film Collection, 200 FC-4304.
20.  Ford Archives, Reminiscences of J. L. McCloud, pp. 381, 387; Marquis, *Henry Ford,* p. 4.


## 8. THE MACHINE IS THE NEW MESSIAH

1.  Marx, *Machine in the Garden,* p. 234. Ralph Waldo Emerson, *Emerson's Essays* (Oxford University Press, 1936), pp. 256, 135-36.
2.  Trine and Ford, *Power That Wins,* p. 144; Henry Ford and Samuel Crowther, *Today and Tomorrow* (New York: Doubleday, Page & Co., 1926), p. 117. "Machinery, the New Messiah" *Forum,* March, 1928, 359.
3.  Malcolm Cowley, *The Faulkner-Cowley File* (New York: Viking Press, 1968), p. 15; allusion to F. Scott Fitzgerald's *The Great Gatsby* (New York: Charles Scribner's Sons, 1953), p. 182. For further information about early metallurgy see the first two chapters of Mircea Eliade's *The Forge and the Crucible* (New York: Harper & Row, 1971).

# BIBLIOGRAPHIC ESSAY

Any Ford bibliography must begin with the seven books he published using various coauthors. All seven appeared in just eight years, beginning in 1922, itself a near proof that Ford could not have done the majority of the work. Four were written by Samuel Crowther under his supervision beginning with *My Life and Work* (New York, 1922), *Today and Tomorrow* (New York, 1926), *Moving Forward* (New York, 1930) and *Edison as I Knew Him* (New York, 1930). None of these may be relied upon without reservations. Ford merely gave Crowther some interviews leaving him and his secretary to fill out details and organize the books. When written all were screened by the publicity department of the company. Nevertheless, the "Autobiography" and the Edison work are valuable if used with caution. Far less useful, *Ford Ideas* (Dearborn, Michigan, 1922) consists entirely of editorials from the *Dearborn Independent* written by others, particularly Cameron and Pipp, in a style quite unlike that of the Crowther volumes. *My Philosophy of Industry* (New York, 1929) reprints interviews which had been published the previous year in *Forum*, but these are not true interviews, appearing in essay form, composed by Fay Leone Farote. In contrast *The Power That Wins* (Indianapolis and New York, 1930) consists of a dialogue between Ralph Waldo Trine and Ford. An important and rare book of over 200 pages, it was obviously smoothed over and edited for publication but retains the essence of his ideas, which must be studied further in numerous early newspaper and magazine interviews.

Most of the vast Ford bibliography consists of books written during his lifetime, which lack critical perspective. These include a spate of popular biographies, mostly from the 1920's; several fictional works which either allude to or directly refer to him; and a number of personal reminiscences by close associates. The popular biographies, while suggestive, are full of misinformation and the quirks of their authors. Most portray Ford as a hero, although a few from the 1930's view him as an oppressor of labor. They provide good source material for contemporary opinions, but they do not begin to summarize the magazine literature, which charts Ford's public image in far greater detail. Some of the better portraits may be found in Gamaliel Bradford's *The Quick and the Dead* (Boston, 1931), Jonathan Norton Leonard's *The Tragedy of Henry Ford* (New York, 1932), and Charles Mertz's *And Then Came Ford* (New York, 1929).

Of the fictional works which deal with Ford, three deserve mention. Aldous Huxley's *Brave New World* (New York, 1932) is discussed in this text. Louis-Ferdinand Celine's *Journey to the End of the Night* (New York, 1964) provides a chilling account of the author's employment at a Ford factory, and E. L. Doctorow's *Ragtime* (New York, 1975) comprehends Ford's religious concerns, albeit largely in jest.

Personal evaluations of Ford, although narrow in focus, are often penetrating. Typically, they grew out of a few years of marginal association with him, but fail to consider the whole sweep of his career. The most valuable are Samuel Marquis's *Henry Ford, an Interpretation* (Boston, 1923) and Charles E. Sorensen's *My Forty Years with Ford* (New York, 1956), although the latter must be cross-examined carefully whenever possible. It was written with assistance from Samuel T. Williamson. Marquis headed the Ford Motor Company's Sociological Department shortly after World War I; Sorensen's ties lasted much longer and the book runs toward self-justification. The following are also useful: Allan Benson, *The New Henry Ford* (New York, 1923) for just after WWI; Charles B. King, *Psychic Reminiscences* (private, 1935) on Ford in the 1890's; Louis P. Lochner, *America's Don Quixote* (London, 1924) on the Peace Ship; H. F. Morton, *Strange Commissions for Henry Ford* (York, England, 1934) on Greenfield Village; E. G. Pipp, *The Real Henry Ford* (Detroit, 1922) on *The Dearborn Independent;* William C. Richards, *The Last Billionaire* (New York, 1948), a reporter's view of Ford in the 1930's and 1940's; and William L. Stidger's worshipful *Henry Ford, the Man and His Motives* (New York, 1923) for the early 1920's. Lastly, William A. Simonds spent most of his life with the Ford Motor Company and his *Henry Ford* (New York, 1943) contains some information but is uncritical.

Scholarly works appeared only after Ford's death. In 1948 Keith Sward's *The Legend of Henry Ford* (1948) attempted a full picture of the man, but as it was written during the final years of Ford's life with the aid of labor union files, the book is sadly biased against him, although it offers numerous insights into both his character and the implications of his life. The most significant scholarship on Ford is still the three volume study by Allan Nevins and Frank Hill: *Ford: The Times, the Man, the Company* (New York, 1954); *Ford: Expansion and Challenge 1915-32* (New York, 1957); and *Ford: Decline and Rebirth* (New York, 1963). This massive work was prepared concurrently with the formation of the Henry Ford Archives, which now include the notes of Nevins and Hill along with all the private Ford papers and business documents.

However, the inclusiveness of the Nevins-Hill study based on these immense resources is also its weakness. Henry Ford himself is largely forgotten during those chapters dealing with competition, business developments, foreign expansion, labor history, and the various types of automobiles. When returning to Ford, these volumes tend to be more descriptive and biographical than analytic. At no point are Ford's principal ideas discussed in detail. Rather, they arise as new situations develop, or recur in spite of their apparent absurdity.

Recent scholars have not studied Ford's system of ideas, but they have used the Archives in such works as Myra Wilkins and Frank Hill's *American Business Abroad: Ford on Six Continents* (Detroit, 1964) and William Greenleaf's excellent *Monopoly on Wheels* (1961), a study of Ford and the Selden Patent. The interest in Ford's biography continued, as Roger Burlingame produced *Henry Ford: A Great Life in Brief* (New York, 1955), and Sidney Olson researched the forgotten years of Ford's life in *Young Henry Ford* (Detroit, 1963). Olson's work is by far the more valuable of the two, drawing upon the Archives and the author's knowledge of local history, while Burlingame's book is largely a collation of previous biographies.

Neither author attempted a full analysis of Ford's character. This task was undertaken, however, by Anne Jardim in *The First Henry Ford: A Study in Personality and Business Leadership* (Cambridge, Mass., 1970). She writes almost entirely from a Freudian perspective, and takes no account of either American intellectual history or Ford's ideas. Even on its narrowly defined psychological ground, however, Jardim's work cannot stand. It completely ignores Ford's relationship with his mother and relies extensively on secondary sources to support a theory which places primary emphasis on the father. She mistakes popular myths about Ford composed in the Horatio Alger vein for authenticated testimony, particularly in the use of Benson and Sorensen, cited above. Her book curiously misreads personal bias and popular myth in her sources, yet does contain some insights into Ford's life. She does not examine his belief in reincarnation.

Most recent scholarship on Ford has focused upon him as a popular figure. Reynold Wik's *Henry Ford and Grass Roots America* (Ann Arbor, Michigan, 1972) surveys thousands of letters written to Ford by rural Americans, preserved in the Archives. This work is a valuable resource, but it fails to master its enormous primary sources and marshall them in an overall pattern, becoming anecdotal in profuse and often hilarious quotations. Wik's focus on Ford's rural support is interesting but he does not demonstrate that his appeal was substantially different for urbanites. Regional differences do not appear crucial in the one previous book that could be included within the American Studies myth and symbol school, Sigmund Diamond's excellent *The Reputation of American Businessmen* (Cambridge, Mass., 1955). He focuses entirely on Ford's image at death in comparison with obituaries of earlier American business leaders.

Two works have attempted to describe the Ford career through study of public images, without making a firm methodological distinction between public symbols and private life. Gordon Westbrook Davidson's unpublished dissertation "Henry Ford: The Formation and Course of a Public Figure" (Columbia University, 1966) argues that Ford was emotional, childish, and inadequately educated for the role he assumed. He explains Ford's continued popularity as an expression of financial power combined with his unusual opinions. This approach necessarily obscures the sharp oscillations in the Ford public image, a problem which also affects David L. Lewis's *The Public Image of Henry Ford: An American Folk Hero and His Company* (Detroit, 1976). Based on a 1959 dissertation concerning Ford's public relations, it is a lavishly illustrated cornucopia of anecdote and detail but is not always critical of its subject. Virtually every unpublished item of importance by or concerning Ford may be found in the Henry Ford Archives. Its 500 accessions fill a mile of shelf space. In addition, it possesses 300 scrap books of newspaper clippings, over 100,000 photographs, banks of files containing magazine articles, and several hundred volumes of reminiscences in an oral history series. In these last testify almost all of Ford's relatives, executives, and friends. A useful collection, particularly for critics of Ford, is the Labor History Archives at Wayne State University. Finally, over 1,500,000 feet of film were presented by the Ford Motor Company to the National Archives in 1963. These are catalogued in Mayfield Bray's 100 page *Guide to the Ford Film Collection* (Washington, 1970). Using that collection, I caught a glimpse of Ford standing in a muddy yard and talking to two unidentified men. They agreed to a jumping contest. Ford made a short, practical jump; the other two tried to beat him and fell in the mud.

# INDEX

Adams, Henry, 39, 85
Anarchist, Ford as, 17–18
Anti-semitism, 28, 72, 89–92, 107, 111, 115
Assembly line, introduction, 14; and workers, 43–44; operation, 74–75; as cultural expression, vii–ix, 125, 127–129
Assimilation of immigrants, 71, 129
Automobile, as social force, vii–ix, 11, 23–24, 71, 74, 77–78, 127–129; see also Model T
Automotive design, 11, 36, 38, 81–82, 100, 108, 120, 126

Bacon, Irving, 97, 117–118
Barton, Bruce, 23
Battle of the Overpass, 50, 116
Bennett, Harry, 45, 115–116, 119
Benson, Allan, 97, 110, 135, 140
Biographies, Ford, 35, 41, 97, 139–143
*Boston Transcript,* 16
Bradford, Gameliel, 35, 140
Brisbane, Arthur, 18
Bryan, William Jennings, 20, 91
Burbank, Luther, 20
Burroughs, John, viii, 20, 67, 82; on Ford, 106–107, 111
Bynner, Witter, 29

Cameron, William, 52, 91, 114, 139; see also *Dearborn Independent*
Capitalism, Ford's idea of, 70, 84–89; see also Ford, economics

Carlyle, Thomas, viii
Cartoons of Ford, 26, 112
Chemurgy, 79–82, 107
*Chicago Herald,* 18
*Chicago Tribune* lawsuit, 17–18; omission of in biographies, 35; effect on Ford, 69, 108–109
Christianity, and public, 22–23, 29–34; and labor, 45, 53; and culture, 129–131
Coal, 75, 83, 115
*Collier's Weekly Magazine,* presidential poll, 25
Communism, see socialism
Competition, automotive, 12–13, 36, 70, 72, 75, 115, 141
Coolidge, Calvin, 22, 28, 35
Crowther, Samuel, 41, 72, 139
Culture and nature, confused, 24–25, 47–49, 82–87, 125–130

Dante, 30–31
*Dearborn Independent,* 27, 72, 89, 109, 140
"Dearborn Massacre," 44–46, 50, 54; Ford view of, 115–116
Detroit, 11, 14, 38, 42, 99–100
Diamond, Sigmund, 55, 142
Dynamic standard of value, 82–86

Ecology, viii, 81–83, 130–131
Edison, Thomas Alva, public figure, viii, 20, 27, 127; and Ford, 73, 83, 100–101, 112, 120, 139

144

Eliade, Mircea, 5, 128, 130
Emerson, Ralph Waldo, and Ford,
 vii–viii, 7, 57, 60, 63, 78, 87,
 93–95, 104, 107, 108; and culture,
 125–126
Energy, 82–87; see also Muscle Shoals
Energy Dollar, 26–27, 85–86

Farm animals, no need for, 78–81
Firestone, Harvey, 20, 67, 83
Fitzgerald, F. Scott, 22, 131
Five Dollar Day, and public, 13–15,
 23, 37; and Ford, 72–73, 107
Ford, Clara, 98, 99, 103, 106
Ford, Edsel, 62, 67, 103, 115
Ford English School, 71
Ford, Henry, apprenticeship, 99;
 beliefs, 59–92, 107–108, 112–113,
 115–118, 128–129; childhood,
 95–99, 117–118; on creativity,
 60–62, 94, 100, 128; death, 55;
 diet, 64–66, 77–78; early invention,
 11–12, 100–103; economic views,
 70–74, 86–92; marriage, 99; pacifism,
 15, 70–71, see also Peace Ship;
 parents, 60, 95–99, 117–118;
 personality, 93–95, 101–105, 107–
 121; as symbol, vii, 3, 9–10, 16–56,
 127–131
Ford, Mary, 96–98, 104; reincarnated,
 116–119
Ford Motor Company, 12, 15, 27, 45,
 65, 71, 74–77, 102, 105
Ford Service Department, 43; see also
 Bennett, Harry
Ford, William, 95–96, 103, 118
Fordism, 51–52
Fortune Magazine, 49
Forum Magazine, 26, 29–30, 41
Freud, Sigmund, 5, 113
Friends of Democracy, 52

General Motors, and Ford, 36, 75;
 and labor, 49–50
Gold standard, 26, 84–87
Gray, John, 12
Greeley, Andrew, 37
Green, Theodore, 4
Greenfield Village, and history, ix,
 63–64; origin, 97–98, 116
Guest, Edgar, 97

Harding, Warren G., 20, 22, 25, 35
Handy, Robert, 22
Hemingway, Ernest, 22

Hill, Frank, see Allan Nevins
History, Ford's sense of, 63–64, 68,
 77–92, 127–129
"History is bunk," 113
Hitler, Adolf, 28, 52, 91
Hood, Anne, 95
Hoover, Herbert, 20, 22
Huxley, Aldous, 41

Ideology, American, 10–11, 48–49,
 125–131; see also pastoralism,
 utopia
"Ignorant idealist," Ford self-styled as,
 18, 69; form of his idealism, 59–63
Illustrated World, 24–25
Industrialization, and culture, 9–11,
 125, 127–128; public and, 14,
 23; Ford on, 74–82

J 8, 43
Jackson, Andrew, as symbol, 4, 10,
 55; and Ford, 86, 88
Jardim, Anne, 95, 106, 137, 141–142
Johansson Blocks, 72
Jokes, Ford, 19

Kahn, Murshid Inayat, 113
Kanzler, Ernest, 62, 76
King, Charles B., 99–100, 140
Knowledge, Ford's idea of, 59–64,
 94, see Reincarnation
Kolko, Gabriel, 70

Leonard, Jonathan, 41, 140
Levi-Strauss, Claude, 5, 56, 130
Lewis, David, 142
Lindberg, Charles, 45, 93
Literary Digest, 18, 22, 24, 26
Lizzie labels, 34
Lochner, Louis, 109–110, 140

McLuhan, Marshall, 71
Marquis, Samuel, and Ford, 62, 72,
 76, 109, 110–111, 114, 140
Marx, Karl, 86–92
Marx, Leo, 47–48
Masons, 96
Mass production, and public, 14–15,
 30–32; and workers, 43–44, 53–54;
 and Ford, 74–77, 125; and society,
 128–129
Merriweather, Richard, 50
Messiah, Ford as secular, 22–23, 29–34,
 36–39, 130–131; machine as, 129
Mexico, 71

*Middletown,* 23

Mobility, 3, 10, 15, 21, 37, 40, 43, 49;
  Ford's view of, 60-61, 67-68

Model A, 38-39, 47, 67, 112

Model T, and consumers, 9, 14-16, 19,
  23, 24, 34, 36-37; as pastoral image,
  47-48; and Ford, 62, 68, 75-76, 79,
  103, 120; and Emerson, 126; and
  culture, 127-129

Moral rearmament, 71-72

Mt. Clemens trial, see *Chicago Tribune*

Muscle Shoals, and public, 24-26,
  35; and Ford, 69, 83-86, 115, 126

*My Life and Work,* 41, 72, 139


*Nation,* the, 17, 25, 35, 36, 41, 45

National Recovery Administration, 42,
  45, 67, 116

Nazism, 52, 91

Nevins, Allan, 62, 103, 115, 141

*New Republic,* 26, 41, 46, 51

New Thought, 107, 112

*New York Daily People,* 14; also see
  Socialism

*New York Globe,* 13

*New York Times,* 13, 65, 74, 81

Newberry, Truman, 16

Nineteen thirties, 40-53, 115-116

Nineteen twenties, 20-39, 48, 109-113

Norris, Senator Frank, 25


Oldfield, Barney, 11

Olson, Sidney, 66, 101, 141

*Only Yesterday,* 22

Ortega y Gasset, 48


Pacificism, 71, 84, 94

Pastoralism, 36, 47-48, 77-79; also
  see Ideology

Peace Ship, and public, 15-16, 35;
  and Ford, 68, 70, 93, 107, 109

Pells, Richard, 43

Pipp, E. G., 72, 139, 140

Poetry about Ford, 29, 33, 51; also
  see songs about Ford

Populism, 16, 91

Precognition, 61, 96-97, 112; also
  see reincarnation

Presidential campaign, Ford's, 25-28,
  88

Profits, 15, 27-28, 87

Prohibition, 66, 74

Public images, 4, 5; also see Ford, as
  symbol

Publicity Department, Ford, 13,
  113-114, 139

Racing, 11

Raushenbush, Carl, 51

Reading, Ford's, viii, 99, 103-104,
  106-108, 112-113

Reed, John, 67, 77

Reincarnation, as belief, 56, 59-63,
  67-68; origin of belief, 103-105; in
  practice, 112, 117-119, 128

Reuther, Walter, 50

River Rouge Plant, 30, 31, 75, 77;
  see also Ford Motor Company

Road steam engine, 98, 116

Rockefeller, John D., 10, 20

Rogers, Will, 93, 106

Roosevelt, Franklin D., 40, 45, 49,
  55, 67

Russia, 9, 70, 87


Sanborn, Frank, 106

Selden Patent, 12, 73, 88

Service ideal, Ford's, 72-74

Sinclair, Upton, 51

Smith, Orlando, 103-104

Socialism, 14, 44, 49, 51; and Ford,
  86-87

Songs, about Ford, 24, 33, 42, 53

Sorenson, Charles E., 76, 115, 140

Soybeans, 65, 79-80

Spencer, Herbert, 95

Stidger, William, 30-32, 54, 140

Strikes, 49-53; Ford's view of, 88-89,
  115-116

Sunday, Billy, 22-23

Swedenborg, Emanuel, 112

Symbol, defined, 3-4


Thoreau, Henry David, 106-107

Time, American view of, 127-130;
  Ford's view of, 103-105, 128-129

*Time Magazine,* 53-54

Tractor, Ford, 17, 19, 27, 79

Trevor-Roper, H. R., 90

Trine, Ralph Waldo, 112, 113, 135, 139

Turner, Frederick Jackson, 10


Unemployment, 40, 44, 89, 120

Unions, see workers

Utopia, industrial, 4, 25, 34, 77-82,
  127-128


Vernacular tradition, 126-127

Village industries, 77-78


Wages, 13, 40-41, 75

*Wall Street Journal,* 13

War profits, 27-28

Ward, John William, 4
Water power, 82–84, see also Muscle
    Shoals
Wayside Inn, 42
White, E. B., 47
Whitman, Walt, 104, 112
Wik, Reynold, 18, 142

Wilson, Edmund, 43, 62
Wilson, Woodrow, 16
Windmills, 83
Workers, 13–14, 24, 40–44, 49–53,
    74–75
World War I, 15–16
World War II, 53–54